Mistresses

Contents

The Mistress: Who Is She?
    p. 1

The Masochist
    p. 9

The Search for a Father Figure
    p. 20

The Scarlet Woman
    p. 33

The Marriage Maker:
Fulfilling the Male Need (1)
    p. 42

The Marriage Maker:
Fulfilling the Male Need (2)
    p. 51

The Male Conflict
    p. 59

The Marriage Breaker
    p. 68

The Sexual Partner
    p. 76

The Mistress Behind the Man
    p. 87

The Predator
    p. 96

The Free Agent
 p. 104
The Failure of Monogamy
 p. 113

Mistresses

The Mistress: Who Is She?

Laura Beame is twenty-five, a journalist who has worked for ABC, UPI and *Newsweek*. Born and raised in Brooklyn, she is attractive, Jewish and unmarried.

Elizabeth Shields is a warm, middle-aged, plain and plumpish woman with a poor skin and frumpy clothes that never seem to fit. She is a policewoman.

Helen Lewis is a married housewife with two children. She is pleasant-looking in a quiet, unassuming way, shy and withdrawn.

Nicole Le Hay is tall with long dark hair, slim, sophisticated, and well dressed.

What do these women, with their disparate lives, who would never under normal circumstances meet, have in common with one another—and with thousands of other women? They are, or have been, mistresses. According to our definition, this means they are (or have been) involved in a long-term relationship with a married man. We chose a year as the minimum period of involvement.

The very nature of the illicit relationships in which all these women are involved makes it difficult to estimate how widespread extra-marital affairs are in society today. Most would deny their involvement to inquiring strangers, be they busybodies or earnest researchers. Kinsey, in his controversial study, *Sexual Behavior of the Human Male*, 1948, estimated that one out of every two married men in the United States was, or had been, involved in extra-marital sex. A more recent study of six thousand American executives, "Executive Lifestyles," concluded that one out of every five businessmen was involved in extra-marital sex. The percentage rises to one out of every three for executives who are away from home for thirteen or more weeks a year.

Whatever the exact numbers involved, it is clear that the extra-marital affair is a widespread, although covert and unacknowledged, phenomenon. The mistress, in contemporary guise, is thriving in American society, even though, amidst current preoccupations with open marriage, de facto marriage, group sex and pre-marital sex, she has so far been largely ignored.

There is no contemporary euphemism for mistress. Yesterday's spinster is today's "swinging single," a childless couple is "child-free," but there is no fashionable word for "mistress." The word still conjures up visions of Mme. de Pompadour reclining on a chaise-longue in the court of Louis XV, or of Emma Hamilton almost persuading Lord Nelson not to fight in the Battle of Trafalgar. To most people, in short, the mistress remains a glamorous figure of the past, the center of intrigue and drama, a coquettish, pampered luxury, the heroine of historical films, romantic novels and Elizabethan plays.

In fact, far from living the glamorous and romantic lives assigned to them by their biographers, most mistresses (even the most notorious, such as Lady Caroline Lamb and Emma Hamilton) probably led a fairly humdrum existence, punctuated by moments of exhilaration and periods of dark despair.

The advent of feminism has wrought drastic changes

in the way the modern mistress sees herself, but the conflicts and ambiguities of the past remain. Like her historic predecessor, today's mistress must still endure the strain of an illicit, clandestine relationship which makes her subordinate to, and often dependent on, a man. Today, however, she no longer has the material advantages that used to come with being "kept." The pampered mistress is the exception. Apart from the "predator" who enters into a relationship for economic gains, most mistresses receive few luxuries and are lucky if they get a bottle of wine and a couple of good meals a week. A man rarely pays for, or helps out with, the rent of an apartment. And most mistresses refuse financial assistance out of pride, because it makes more blatant the reality they would prefer to avoid: that they are mistresses.

The very word has become, for most women, pejorative. The masculine equivalent—"lover"—has a positive ring to it. But the word "mistress" joins the string of derogatory terms that have been used throughout history to describe women—prostitute, harlot, whore, fallen woman, scarlet woman—and sums them up.

The mistress-lover relationship was built on a double standard. The man *had* a mistress, who was presumed to exist only in relation to him. Part of the outrage that accompanied the publication of D. H. Lawrence's book *Lady Chatterley's Lover* may have been the role reversal implied in the title. The word "mistress" suggests that a woman has a "master," that she is the possession of a male.

The Victorian days of the "kept" woman may be over, but while the contemporary mistress is no longer financially owned by her lover, she is normally expected to be his emotionally. The double standard still prevails, with the lover often expecting total fidelity from his mistress while assuming his right to be as unfaithful as he likes.

In the past, the mistress was there to satisfy the emotional and sexual needs of her lover. Her needs were rarely taken into consideration. It was the classic situation of dominance and subordination. Only a few mistresses, such as Lady Conyngham (mistress to George IV) and Mme. de Pompadour, learned to turn the situation to their own advantage.

Although increasing numbers of mistresses today are discovering advantages in extra-marital affairs (the "free agent," the "predator," the "woman-behind-the-man"), the majority (the "masochist") have yet to break out of the classic subordinate role.

A mistress, even the "predatory" mistress, cannot escape society's condemnation. She is a woman who is committing the crime of adultery. If she is in love, she is still considered to be committing a crime, because she loves a married man. So the fulfillment that is expected to come from being in love is denied her.

Whatever her feelings toward her lover, the mistress remains a transgressor in the eyes of the public. Either she gives in to the pressures of society and sacrifices her love in the name of public morality, or she gives in to her feelings and becomes an outsider. Whichever road she takes, she will probably find suffering and anguish along the way. The fact that she can only blame herself will make it worse.

The "wronged" wife always has someone else to blame. The breakdown of her marriage can be attributed to forces beyond her control—her isolation, lack of stimulation, her husband's infidelity, and so on. It is difficult for the mistress to project her guilt onto anyone else.

Most mistresses are marriage-makers rather than marriage-breakers, but this aspect of their role is rarely recognized. Being or having a mistress continues to be the most taboo of extra-marital activities.

When we set out to find mistresses to interview, friends and acquaintances told us that we were embarking on an impossible task. But in fact we had no trouble finding more than the forty women for our sample. Our interviews were conducted in Great Britain and the United States and included, in addition to women from these two countries, women from Canada, Germany, Holland, Ireland, Australia and New Zealand.

Our preconceptions of a mistress as a glamorous single woman were rapidly shattered as we found ourselves talking to an extremely varied cross section of female society. Although the norm is still a single woman, and a fairly attractive single woman at that, we interviewed women who could only be described as plain, withdrawn, nervous, and awkward. What they did have in common was that they were primarily "middle class." All but three were involved in some professional occupation, although eleven came originally from "working class" backgrounds. They worked in journalism, publishing, the academic world and medicine; they were secretaries and office girls. Four were housewives. The ages of the women ranged from twenty-two to fifty-five, with the majority in the twenty-five to thirty-five age bracket. Two mistresses had had children by their lovers.

The personalities of the male lovers were as varied as their looks. Six could only be described as plain, three as "attractive," three as "handsome." Some were involved in journalism, publishing, advertising, the mass media. One was a lawyer, one owned a small factory, one was a traveling salesman, one was a university professor and one a politican (all occupations where there is considerable opportunity for them to meet single or available women).

The men's ages ranged from the early thirties to the late forties. Of the fifty men and women we interviewed, forty had met their mistresses or masters at work, or in some related activity—a social function, for example.

Time and economics make the modern mistress a middle-class luxury. The man who can most conveniently have a mistress, according to one of our informed male lovers, is a wealthy businessman working erratic hours, married to a woman preoccupied with children and inured to her husband's prolonged "business trips." We interviewed twelve men and all were financially well off. All but two had "legitimate" reasons for being away from home constantly. These two saw their mistresses immediately after work (the five-to-seven dash) and built up their emotional relationship during office hours. Six men had begun or continued their affairs with women in the same office.

There was dramatic variation in the length of the involvements. One affair had lasted for twenty-seven years, six had lasted for seven to ten years, five for six years, and the rest between one and four years. In fact three of the long-term affairs had been going for as long as the parallel marriages. Given that most of the lovers' meetings took place two or three times a week on the average (as well as at work in some cases) it is obvious that most affairs were very deep. They were not passing fancies, but clearly filled a need, for in hourly terms most of our sample spent as much time with their mistresses each week as they did with their wives. Some relationships had evolved into marriage without title, always with the difference that they were devoid of the stresses and social acceptance of recognized marriages.

Most of the relationships developed in a rather

cloistered world. The mistresses and their lovers lived separate lives with little overlap between them except for the intense moments together. In a hothouse situation like this, feelings of infatuation which drew the lovers together in the beginning could be sustained for a long period of time. When they met they could concentrate exclusively on each other without interference from the normal encumbrances of a marriage. Such relationships have all the fantasy ingredients—excitement, knife-edged insecurity and secrecy.

We have preserved the anonymity of our sample because there was always a third person involved, either the wife or the husband. Several wanted to stand up and be counted—mistresses, that is—because they saw no reason why they should hide or be embarrassed by their relationships. But in the interest of the other mistresses who felt insecure or self-conscious and awkward in their role, they accepted our decision not to publish names or give clues that might lead to their identity being revealed.

One of the effects of feminism has been to enable women to see their problems and difficulties as common experiences arising out of prevailing social (and sexist) conditions. Women have gained strength and support by sharing their experiences in consciousness-raising groups, feminist organizations, magazines and the ever-growing feminist press.

Other socially suspect minority groups (such as lesbians) have managed to band together to help each other, but there is no literature or organized movement in which the mistress can share her experiences or see herself honestly reflected. Her problems and her ambivalences remain mysteries. As former mistresses ourselves, we have written this book for these isolated women and their lovers in the hope that it will offer some insight into the extra-marital relationship, the possibility of which, at least, will present itself to almost every man and woman in our society at some stage of their lives.

The Masochist

Beverly White is thirty-five but looks twenty-five. A former model, she is thin, nervous, with a constantly worried expression. She works as an executive secretary in a leading New York commercial firm.

"When I last had an affair with a married man, I had a low—I mean, really low—image of myself. I thought of myself as a monumental failure—as a woman, as a career woman, as a human being. I had had a dreadful series of affairs over the last four or five years which had left me feeling depressed and debased. They were really sordid relationships, and I was feeling so abused at this stage of my life that when this man turned up and said to me 'I want you to know that I love you,' that was enough. Once again, I fell madly in love.

"I mean, here I was sickened by the crassness and insensitivity of the men I had recently been involved with, when all of a sudden this marvelous man turns up. He was married but that seemed the only thing wrong with him. He realized that I had a mind and a brain and he appreciated me for it. He was a success and I was your arch-failure, so I fell for him.

"He explained to me right away that he had a really bad marriage. When I found out what he was going through with his wife I said to myself, eventually he'll cut ties with her. I'll just sit around waiting and making myself indispensable, and eventually he'll realize that I am indispensable, and bingo—he'll marry me.

"It was a part-time relationship, but I was ready to accept that. He would come in late at night and I would have a meal waiting for him. I never made any demands on him. I never asked, when am I going to see you next, or what time will you be in for dinner? After all, what right did I have to ask him that?

"I was a failure, and the only way I could cease to be a failure, I thought, was if I eventually married this man who was a success.

"Well, pretty soon I began to realize he wasn't quite as wonderful as I had first thought. He was paranoid about his wife's finding out—I mean, *totally* paranoid. If we went into a restaurant he'd be looking over his shoulder to make sure there was no one he knew there—and you know what that makes you feel like—like a piece of dirt. Nowadays I would walk out on a man who did that, but in those days I never opened my mouth. I went along with it all. This is the way it is, I said to myself. Don't rock the boat, after all, you're a failure, you haven't a leg to stand on; you've no right to open your mouth or make demands. Be nice—don't be a bitch.

"He was very unimaginative and insensitive as a lover, and again, in bed, he managed to make me feel like a piece of dirt. He was always saying, have you washed yourself? Are you clean? You didn't spend much time in the bathroom. Sometimes I would go to the bathroom and cry, but then I would say to myself, this is something I've got to get over. It's the price I must pay for marrying this man. I'll just have to adjust to this feeling that I'm dirt. And he made it very clear that he felt he was doing something dirty, something sinful, especially because he was always dashing off as soon as we'd finished making love—if that's what you could call it. He wouldn't even stay the night with me when his wife was out of town. He was so paranoid that he thought someone from his office might see him on the subway and realize he was coming in a different direction from his home.

"Gradually it got more and more part-time. He was always having business dinners to go to, or so he said. Also, his wife was a real bitch, the way she treated him. She was constantly ordering him around, telling him to pick up packages for her, pick her up after work, and so on. And all the time she was sleeping with other men and being quite blatant about it. It dawned on me gradually that she was dishing out this sadistic stuff to him and he was lapping it up from her and then taking it out on me. In other words, he was punishing me for her treatment. Once, later on, I said to him—'you know, she gets the meat, you get the potatoes, and I get the skins.' That was the arrangement, he snapped back.

"But I never thought of myself as being masochistic at the time, putting up with all that shit, because I never imagined it would be permanent. I thought I would just go along with it for a while, and once he got the new house, or his new job—there was always some pretext—then he'd have more time for me, and it would all get better. Just another couple of months, I would say to myself, just a little while longer, and eventually it will all straighten itself out.

"I really wanted to marry him, because I thought you weren't really a woman until you were a wife. It was the old pattern—you want something so much you forget what it is you really wanted in the first place. You lose your perspective. I wanted him so much I forgot the fact that he couldn't possibly have supplied me with what I wanted in a marriage. There was no trust or faith in the relationship at all, but I couldn't see further than my obsession to get him to consider rationally what would happen if I eventually did.

"Not that there was much chance of that. When I finally faced up to the fact that this "interim situation," as I liked to think of it, was in fact permanent, I finished the affair. That was two years after it had started. I felt extremely bitter about it, and still do. I didn't really get any pleasure or ego-reinforcement from it at all. It only further convinced me of my inadequacy. I realize that with men, it's business and their balls first, the kids next, then the wife, then finally, way down at the bottom of the pile, after the neighbors and the relatives and all that, comes the mistress. Once everything else is taken care of, a man will throw her a few skins to chew on.

"Now I ask myself, why do I need another affair? Why do I need all that *angst*? The kind of happiness you get from an affair is so terribly temporary and insecure, and afterward you feel so awful, that it's simply not worth it. I feel I've been through it all and paid my dues. I've been abused and humiliated by men and I don't need any more of it. I know what to expect from an affair with a married man. I see the pattern now—I've been through it all before, and I know how it's going to end.

"I met a man at a real estate course I took recently who was beautiful and desirable—but married. He wanted to hop into bed with me, of course, but I said to him, get rid of your wife first, then I'll sleep with you. We remain friends but I know he'll never leave his wife. He keeps telling me he's going to get a divorce, that he's just got to get a bit more money, or spend one more summer with the kids, but I know he'll never leave. I know all the stories, and I know he's not going to leave her till he's carried out on a stretcher, or in a hundred years' time, when I'm a little old lady. So what's the point? My rule of thumb now is, if I can't get more positives than negatives, forget it. I don't believe in love and romanticism any longer. The high point of an affair is usually the first night; after that it's all downhill. None of my affairs has lasted, so now I don't expect any future ones to. I don't expect to get married or even to have a decent relationship. Why should it happen now if it hasn't happened before? I'm much more difficult now. I refuse to play games any longer, or sit around taking all the shit. I'm never going to accept the 'I can't-be-seen-with-you-because-people-might-recognize-me' syndrome. Nor am I going to accept business dinners as an excuse. If that means I've got to live by myself with my cats for the rest of my life and be lonely, then that's just what it means."

Those mistresses involved in relationships which brought them more unhappiness and misery than enjoyment and fulfillment we termed "masochists," since, in varying degrees, the suffering these women experienced seemed to have become almost a necessary part of the affair, if not a source of perverse pleasure and satisfaction. Although Beverly White may be an extreme example, we found that the majority of mistresses we interviewed shared her situation to some extent. Her experience, in fact, can be seen as a paradigm of the mistress-lover relationship.

Inherent in the mistress's situation is a considerable amount of frustration and anxiety. Always number two (if not number four or five, as Beverly White suggested), she has to endure at best a part-time, illicit relationship, and few women are able to survive, let alone thrive on, the emotional, sexual and social tensions that arise when uncertainty, secrecy and dishonesty are forced to become a way of life. The inherent discontinuity of an affair, which is almost always a source of anxiety and insecurity, ensures that whatever the degree of a woman's commitment and self-sacrifice, she will receive in return only partial affection, partial commitment, partial loyalty and a part-time presence.

The satisfaction and love to be derived from this less-than-ideal situation depend to a great extent on the expectations and perceptions both partners bring into a relationship—especially the mistress. If she is seeking to transform the affair into a permanent marriage, then she is likely to wind up frustrated and miserable. If she feels guilty, if she accepts the public version of herself as someone who is doing something sinful, she is likely to judge herself harshly and believe she deserves contempt and abuse. If she becomes totally dependent on her lover emotionally, socially and psychologically, she is likely to end up isolated and lonely, miserably clinging to her lover as the vicarious (and largely absent) center of her existence.

As one mistress observed:

"The more deeply involved the mistress is and the more dependent she is on her lover, the more likely she is to get hurt. All the stresses of the situation—your own guilt, feelings of resentment, the imperative for secrecy, your need of him when you can't have him—all these stresses are compounded as the relationship gets deeper. It gradually gets worse, not better."

The Masochist

Above all, if she has no self-esteem and believes herself to be a failure, she is likely to see the pain and suffering as her "just deserts." One mistress, who realized this only in retrospect, explained:

"If I'd been a stronger and happier person, I would have walked out earlier instead of letting myself be used as I did. I effectively became a second wife to him. He had made me believe he would marry me, so I gave up my job, my friends, my apartment. I literally gave up everything for him. I was a fool."

In such a situation a mistress will often avoid the truth with fantasies and rationalizations. One woman, whose notoriously unfaithful lover demanded total fidelity of her, explained that she refused to believe he could possibly be unfaithful, and had rationalized his prolonged absences and postponed dates for more than two years.

An amazing number of women we interviewed had managed to convince themselves, often in total defiance of the facts, that their lovers were going to leave their wives and settle down with them. Such women, like Beverly White, will often endure extraordinarily cruel and selfish behavior because they are so intent on "getting" their lovers as husbands. They come to center their lives completely around their absentee-lovers, taking themselves and their own feelings less and less into account. Often they will subjugate themselves completely, realizing only later, if at all, what such subjugation entails.

"I was utterly miserable during my entire time with him. He was completely possessive. I wasn't allowed any friends, so I finally gave almost all of them up. I had to, because if I even went to have a drink with one of them

he would become insanely jealous and insist I was having an affair. Yet I spent most of my time outside the office (we worked together) sitting around waiting for him to come and see me.

"I can't remember enjoying myself at all. I had no say in my life, yet in a way I think that was what I wanted, or thought I needed. I had never had any discipline and I wanted his authority. When I did recognize how much it was hurting me, I couldn't take it anymore, so I packed my bags and took off to the other side of the world."

Most, of course, don't take off. Five mistresses recognized the masochism in their behavior, yet felt they were unable or incapable of doing anything about it. Often, the masochistic mistress cannot change the pattern of her existence. Lacking confidence in herself she absorbs and internalizes the stress and pain for which she often has no outlet other than her occasional fits of rage with her lover.

"Because of the intensity of our involvement it was incredibly difficult for me to accept the limitations of the relationship, the possibility that it might end at any time. The deeper the relationship becomes the more time you want to spend with the man and the harder it is not seeing him for long periods of time. These frustrations place new stresses on the whole affair. It becomes a vicious circle."

Whenever she becomes dependent on her lover, she will be plagued by fears of losing him. Her only security is the relationship, however chaotic and unsatisfactory. If her lover has become her whole life and she has discarded friends and other social contacts for him, then she will continually be thinking of ways to kill time, to get her through those anxious and expectant hours before she sees him again.

Even if she has not reached this extreme, the mistress will usually find herself limiting her social availability. Because it *is* a partial, part-time relationship she will have to cancel engagements, put off making dates in advance—just in case her lover might want to see her that night. If she is not available, who knows when he will be free again?

She will find herself waiting for the phone to ring, knowing that she cannot, under any circumstances, telephone her lover, because once he has left their meeting place he enters a world in which she would be an intruder. Even if she's feeling lonely or ill, she cannot rely on her lover's being there to comfort her. She can only sink into misery and self-pity.

"Loneliness gets to bug you. You sit home on a Saturday night, watching another television movie. I was emotionally dependent on my lover, and because we were so close I wasn't getting to meet other people at all. I felt I was vegetating—becoming an old woman at the age of twenty-eight."

Another mistress explained:

"Ours was a very loving relationship, but I used to get terribly frustrated when I wanted to talk to him and he wasn't around. If I was really desperate I could usually get hold of him, but it was unbelievably complicated—ringing friends who ring friends, that sort of thing. During weekends there was absolutely no way of getting hold of him, so I used to go away a lot, just to give myself something to do, to get him off my mind."

Unlike wives and girlfriends, the mistress does not have someone to show off to her friends and family, though they are very likely to be aware, by her continual refusals of invitations and by her excuses, that something is going on. The mistress does not have someone to give her social acceptability and security.

But the most galling aspect of all for the mistress who has become deeply attached to her lover is the knowledge that she must share—physically and emotionally—the man she loves. Conditioned to seek exclusive and symbiotic love, most women find the sharing of a lover especially chafing.

"I know the priorities in his life are, in this order, his work, his child, whom he loves and in whom he sees himself immortalized, his wife, and then me. I'm not stupid enough to think he would ever leave his wife and child, but when he does talk about going away on holiday with his wife I do feel ugly and resentful. He knows I'm after a committed relationship, and when he thinks I'm getting too involved he'll deliberately cool it. When I went into the affair I knew I would get hurt, and I did. I am still being hurt, yet I am still involved."

It is not surprising, given the odds stacked against a mistress in an extra-marital affair, that many go through periods of depression and psychological breakdown, sometimes even attempting suicide. The sad irony is that the more frustrated the mistress is, the more demanding and irritable she becomes, and the more likely it is that she will drive her lover away. Some men disappear as soon as any real pressure or conflict arises. Burdened already with one set of responsibilities, the last thing they want is another.

Many explanations have been offered for masochistic

behavior, ranging from a desire to be punished in order to alleviate unconscious childhood guilt to a conviction that, given her own failure and inadequacy, the mistress deserves to be abased and abused. Whatever the reason, if she doesn't learn from the experience of being hurt and doesn't understand the reasons for her involvement in a masochistic affair, she is likely to repeat her experience until she is caught up in an endless pattern of affairs which leave her increasingly bitter and despairing. As one mistress caught up in such a pattern explained:

"It's when you're feeling at your lowest that you are most vulnerable to getting involved again. I had the normal doubts when I found out my present lover was married. I said to myself, not again—playing second fiddle, never being able to phone him or talk to him when I'm low, not being able to get hold of him. But I was having a lean time and was at my lowest point."

Most mistresses we interviewed, however, were adamant that they would never again repeat the experience—even if it meant giving up relationships with men altogether.

One mistress, summing up, put it this way:

"I know the relationship I had was masochistic. I'm still recovering from it. A stronger and happier person would have walked out much earlier. It must have been conditioned into me to put up with things that bring pain. I gave up a lot for it. I gave up the job I loved, I gave up many of my friends, and I suppose that during the four years I was with him he also prevented me meeting a man I might have married. I shaped my life around him. I'd never do it again."

The Search for a Father Figure

A former model and now a real estate agent, **Lillian Sutch** is thirty-five years old, short, slightly plump, with a somewhat old-fashioned but invariably friendly air about her.

"I lost my father when I was two and I never did remember him. I grew up in an almost exclusively female household—I had no uncles, and my only brother died when I was eight. In adolescence I felt a terrific longing for a father, and although I gradually adjusted to the lack, it left me with an absurdly idealized image of men. They always say the primary influence on a girl's life is her father—his presence or absence—and how he treated her will affect her relationships with men for the rest of her life. Well, the way it affected me was that I totally idealized men. I have spent my whole life looking for a surrogate father—a man who resembled the image I had formed from one worn-out photo of him my mother gave me as a child. The man had to be perfect: noble, strong, dependable and kind—everything I thought a father should be.

"I told a man once that he looked like my father and he said, oh, my God, you're after an incestuous relationship with your absent father, and I said no, not at all, all I want is a man to belong to, and somebody to belong to me. But I know deep down that however much I

The Search for a Father Figure

rationalize it, I am still looking for my father. I'm sure I will never find him, but I don't think I'll ever stop looking.

"When I was twenty-four and still a virgin I went to Paris to model. I was utterly ecstatic to be going there. The second week I met an older man—a well-known movie producer—and we immediately became infatuated with each other. It was all like an Audrey Hepburn movie. I remember walking down the Champs Élysées after this fantastic party and asking him naïvely if he had ever been married. He said yes, for twenty years, and my whole world seemed to collapse.

"But he was extremely attractive, twenty years older than I, debonair, bright—all the things you could ever want in a man. Being a naïve young girl, I was very much in awe of him, not only because of what he was, but also because of *who* he was and all the frills that went along with it. He was very attentive and had an aura about him. He really knew how to treat women, so I was terribly impressed and managed to overcome my puritan inhibitions about having an affair with a married man. I rationalized to myself that he was a marvelous man to go out with and learn all the ropes from so that I would be ready when Prince Charming finally made his appearance.

"He was very straightforward about the fact that he was married. I suppose it would have been difficult to have hidden it, because he was so well known. I saw him on and off for three years—whenever he came to Paris. I consciously tried not to fall too much in love with him, not to fantasize and idealize him as I have all other men I've been involved with, and above all, not to develop expectations that anything might come out of it—I mean, that we would get married or anything. This saved me from getting too hurt, but it also prevented a deep relationship. From the outset I had to exclude the possibility of that, which meant that although on the surface it was very romantic and exciting—strolling down Parisian sidewalks hand in hand, going to marvelous museums, dinners at Maxim's, and so on—ultimately it was as unsatisfactory as all of my affairs have been, because it was superficial and devoid of real commitment.

"I have to admit that deep down I want to be taken care of and protected. I look for somebody stronger, better, more intelligent than I am—often an authority figure like a boss—and idealize him to such an extent that he cannot help but fall short of my expectations. With this first affair I was so much in awe of him, and saw him so intermittently, that there was never time for those expectations to be shattered. The affair ended, ironically, when he fell in love with another woman, divorced his first wife and remarried. I was consumed with jealousy for his second wife, whereas I had never been jealous of his first. I hadn't really thought about her or felt she was a threat. She was a mere shadowy stereotype, whereas this new woman was someone he liked more than me, and that hurt. But I got over it. It was my very first relationship and in a way it set the pattern for all the others. But my affair with him did give me some ego-reinforcement. I lacked an identity of my own, other than a model-girl one, and I have always looked to the men I've had affairs with to provide it for me.

"I've been to psychiatrists who say that part of my idealized self-image is this perfect man. I've always wanted to escape from myself and the world into the arms of my longed-for father. If I had a father or could find a satisfactory substitute, then all my problems, I persuaded myself, would magically disappear.

"So I've always wanted a man with no weaknesses. Whenever I discovered any evidence of weakness I would shrink away. If he wasn't in control, for example, or if he was excessively emotional—if he cried or got very upset—I couldn't stand it. Possibly I wanted them all to be perfect to make up for my own imperfections—though I always labored at making myself into Miss Perfect. If a man mentioned Van Gogh to me, then I knew all about Van Gogh—and Impressionism as well. If he said he would like to go to an opera, then I would rush out and get the best tickets. I could speak French fluently, I could cook superbly—anything I thought Miss Perfect would be able to do.

"Another important influence on my affairs was my mother's subtle insistence that men should be used as a means to climb the social scale. I couldn't possibly get involved with somebody ordinary. He had to be fantastic, which was why I was so passionate about my first movie producer. He had to bring me success and even fame, which I was taught could only be acquired through a man. It was all very confused because deep down, despite this, part of me never expected to get married. What with my father's disappearing when I was young, and my brother's dying, relationships with men seemed transient, and now I don't believe any relationship will last. I expect them all to end. I see couples happily married for fifty years and one part of me says, That's what I really want, while another part of me says even more insistently, That's not possible. I've always tended to shy away from making personal commitments, probably for the very reason that I'm sure relationships aren't going to last. I protect myself from being hurt and rebuffed that way. So perhaps the fact that with married men I knew there weren't going to be great demands made upon me in terms of real commitments nurtured the relationships.

"With the exception of my first affair with a married

man, I've always felt let down at some point in the affair. After the initial euphoria I've always had the feeling that either the men have lost much of their attractiveness, or perhaps it just wasn't there in the first place.

"I've always gone for older men, because you think you know right off who they are. They're not forming their characters—they are what they are, so you think you know where you stand. Not like younger men who are still learning to crawl and walk, who are still feeling their way in the world, like babies.

"I doubt my capacity to have enduring relationships with any man, but perhaps the real reason is that I place such impossible expectations on myself and the men I'm attracted to. I mean, can any man measure up to a lost father?"

Much has been written about the emasculating consequences of a close relationship between a dominant mother and her son. The Portnoy character is a familiar figure in literature and psychological works. But little has been said about the consequences of a close relationship between a dominant father and his daughter, or of the effect of a father's absence on a young girl.

We frequently found in our interviews that the search for a father continues in adulthood in the guise of a search for a mate. Even those women who had extra-marital affairs for economic reasons were often looking for a surrogate father. Not one of the women in our research was involved with a man of her own age, and the age differences ranged from five to twenty-five years. In all but one case the man held a more responsible job than the woman, and he usually maintained a position of considerable power.

One mistress said:

"Having an affair with my lover was like having an affair with the King, the Pope, Charlie Chaplin and my father. It all happened ten years ago, but even now I remember clearly how I simply couldn't stop myself getting involved with him. And at the same time I was absolutely petrified of him."

The irrational, almost masochistic fashion in which she was drawn into this ten-year affair reveals the unconscious motives behind her "choice." Building on Freud's ideas, the psychologist C. G. Jung, who explored the unconscious motives underlying deep emotional relationships, concluded that these often derive from an unconscious tie to a parent. If a woman felt a deep love as a child for her father, she might become jealous of her mother, who prevented her from enjoying an exclusive relationship with him. In later life, Jung points out, such a woman may unconsciously strive to take a man (her father) away from his wife (her mother) in an attempt to recreate and overcome this childhood pattern.

One woman, who through psychotherapy had gained considerable insight into the motives behind her pattern of involvements with married men, explained:

"What I was really trying to do was to take my father away from my mother, and I had spent most of my childhood in unsuccessful attempts. I loved my father and wanted him. I would get him for a while, but never completely. For example, he would take me to a football game. I would go off with him, try to please him and give

my best. But then we'd come home and he'd disappear with my mother, after complaining about her to me, and I couldn't understand it. Here I was longing for my father and there he was in the room next to mine, jiggling on the bed with my mother. So the joy, the satisfaction, when I grew up, of taking a man away from his wife was tremendous. I loved it. I would see a man and immediately go after him. I always succeeded. There was, I realize in retrospect, ferocious jealousy between me and my mother. We were both competing for my father, and ultimately it was I who lost out. So I got my revenge later on in my life, on other men's wives."

Another woman who had been through analysis was equally candid:

"My father seemed so perfect to me as a child that I was left feeling that I could only love a perfect man. I had to get a man who was as good as, or preferably better than, he was, an impossible task, but one which nevertheless sent me careening after corporation heads, successful politicians, and other fantasy figures. I frantically tried to turn myself into a perfect woman—a sort of brilliant, glamorous cliché. I lay in wait for the perfect man who would one day come striding down Fifth Avenue, the answer to all my childhood dreams and fantasies. Since I realized, deep down, that I was never going to get this perfect man, who was of course my father, I went after unattainable men. Being married was a necessary feature. That way I could love a man passionately and avoid facing up to the fact that I never believed I could ever really keep him. The reason, I rationalized, wasn't that I was not good enough, but that he was unattainable, like

The Search for a Father Figure

my father, with a wife who was 'number one' in his life, as my mother had been in my father's life."

Another woman who had grown up with an idealized image of her father described how this had affected the course of her life:

"I grew up with a totally unrealistic picture of my father. I realize now that he's not perfect, far from it, but I still haven't quite taken it in. He embodied all the qualities I admired, and I suppose I've always been looking for those in the men I've gone out with. On the other hand, I never really felt I could measure up to him, even though the standards he set were never made explicit to me—they were only implied. So I was always setting myself impossibly high standards to try to please him—or the father figures I've had affairs with. My whole life has been dedicated to making him (and my lovers) proud of me. My mother was very much a secondary figure in my life. I felt she was inferior intellectually to my father and I reacted against her later on. Eventually part of me began rebelling against my father, too, I guess because I resented my extreme dependence on him. My whole life has been a complicated and impossible exercise to gain his attention and make him proud of me, and now I feel very resentful of that."

One woman whose father had left her mother for a mistress had convinced herself that men loved mistresses, not wives, and had therefore been a mistress for the past ten years. Another woman whose father, like Lillian Sutch's, had left her mother soon after she was born found herself seeking him in every man. From her mother's description she had a picture of him in her mind's eye, and if any man measured up she immediately responded sexually to him.

"I feel I am trying to prove that if I had been my mother my father would not have left. I don't want to believe he left because of me—I have to believe he went away because of something my mother did. My lover tries very hard to understand this obsession of mine, but it places a large burden on our relationship. Sometimes I feel I'll never find happiness until I actually find my father."

Not all mistresses were as explicit as this, nor did all of them specifically mention their fathers, but when describing their lovers they constantly stressed the respect and admiration they had for them, the recognition they had for their power and influence.

"My three lovers have all been very similar. They were all older than me, extraordinarily successful, self-confident and intelligent. I admired and respected them all, both as people and for the positions they held. I realize now that they all resembled my father to an uncanny degree. He was a very strong man who had a great deal of influence over me—and still does."

Particularly if a woman described herself as being independent and self-confident, she made a point of mentioning the difficulty she had in finding someone of her own age she could "look up to."

"The trouble is, the best men in New York are invariably married. It always works out that way. The

men I'm attracted to are articulate, mature, strong, intelligent, have a savoir-faire about life . . . and are married. All the men I've gone out with since the time I first began to date have been at least ten years older than me. My own age holds no attraction for me at all. It may be an Oedipal complex I haven't resolved yet. I had an intense love-hate relationship with my father. It remains so to this day. He's a very dominating man, with a subordinate wife, and three daughters over whom he exercised enormous influence."

Many appeared to be seeking a partner who would dominate them, or at least whom they couldn't dominate: somebody they could ultimately depend on. Hence the attraction to men who are older, more experienced—and married.

"My whole upbringing was geared toward making me independent, and I am very independent in some respects. Financially I am totally independent—I have never been kept. I simply will not allow a man to support me. My pride won't let me. Yet in terms of a man-woman relationship, I like a man to be somewhat domineering. I like to feel I could depend on a man if I had to. I like to feel he has a strong say in the relationship. I want someone I can respect, someone who is strong, someone who can handle any situation. Such people are, without exception, married."

Kindness and understanding come high on the list of sought-after qualities, especially for those women who said they wanted to be looked after and taken care of, again in what was manifestly a paternal way.

"He managed his life with ease. He never seemed to be bothered by anything that went wrong—the meal not being ready on time, my arriving late, that sort of thing. When I was feeling low he'd cuddle me and soothe me. He always seemed to know exactly what I was feeling. I knew that any decision he made would be the right one and I left the organization of the affair to him."

Another woman explained:

"If I was sick and needed comfort, he was someone who could nurse me, someone who was dependable and familiar. He's an important emotional support. The fact that he's older and has strength in areas that I haven't means he can push me where I don't believe in myself. He represents security to me."

In some cases mistresses had allowed themselves to be dominated in the hope that such treatment would ultimately help them to grow and develop—even if this domination was cruelly exercised.

"He was an absolute bastard, but he taught me so much. I think I looked on him as my mother looked on her husband. He was a bastard, but he transformed her from a naïve girl to a talented woman. I thought my lover would do the same for me. I was totally miserable through the whole affair—and yet in a way that was exactly what I wanted."

Another commented:

"I did consider myself a mistress. By that I mean somebody who takes up with a married man but who is removed from his ordinary life, someone who participates in an intense relationship outside the real world. The two have separate lives, separate houses and separate worlds. I was like a simultaneous wife, and those ten years of our involvement were as important and valid as any bad marriage.

"But I got other rewards from the relationship. He brought me up in effect. He was twenty years older than me, and the way he treated me forced me to find out about myself. I learned a lot about how tough life can be. After my cloistered upbringing I needed to learn that."

The search for the father figure is frequently painful and anxiety-ridden, as well as elusive. For the love of a father, unlike the unconditional love of a mother, is traditionally only 'deserved' or 'won' by living up to fatherly expectations. If a woman transfers her frantic childhood desire to please from her father to her lover and interprets this as love, she will probably feel as insecure and anxious as she does passionate, since in the mistress, as in the child, a perpetual effort to please gives rise not only to exhaustion but also to doubts and fears— "If I do not please continually will his love disappear?"

"I realize that instead of simply loving him and being myself, I was putting all my energy into trying to please him and win his admiration. I had no energy or time to think about myself or my feelings, and it never crossed my mind that he should please me also. Ultimately it was a very one-sided relationship."

Bitterness and a feeling of inadequacy understandably accompany this endless search for approval. The woman realizes that she is not loved for herself, but only because she pleases. If the love is withdrawn and the ego is further eroded she may conclude that she has not been loved at all, but only used.

The Scarlet Woman

Joan Gardner is a thirty-year-old Australian journalist who now lives and works in London. She is a confident, dynamic, forceful woman who looks capable of dealing with her problems with ease.

"You can go on for ages doing things that are frowned upon, but it's only when you are found out that the trouble really starts. I must have been very naïve, I think. I'd had two affairs with married men, and they had started and finished without anyone's being in any way aware that anything was amiss. Order was not disturbed, as they say.

"With my third affair it was different. I fell in love and he loved me in return. The problem was that he was a major public figure and I was a threat to his future career. We had six glorious months before the rumors about us started. We'd been seen somewhere together and 'a very good friend' had phoned his wife to tell her.

"I knew all along it was a mistake to go out openly. I had accepted at the beginning that the relationship had to be clandestine, but my lover couldn't bear to have his life prescribed. He said his marriage was finished anyway and that he and his wife were only together because of the children, and because, as a prospective office-holder, people preferred you to be married. As far as the voters were concerned, it didn't matter if the marriage was rotten.

"His wife took the news very badly. She may not have been getting along with her husband, but she had a position to keep up and she had been offended that he didn't feel the same way.

"The next few months were a nightmare. She started spreading rumors about me—she knew who I was but we'd never met. As fast as my friends would deny that I had illegitimate children, that I had been married before, that I was a known prostitute, a new rumor would have started. There was no way of countering them all, apart from taking an ad in the local paper, and that would have meant playing her game.

"I started to feel very self-conscious, paranoiac, about this woman rumor had created. Perhaps I really was a terrible person. I felt guilty that I was in love and I was uncertain about what I should do. The decision was made for me by the people I worked for. I was asked to find another job. Just like that, with no reason given. I found out later that it had been my lover's aide who had arranged the firing. He felt I was a threat to the party, that my lover wouldn't be reelected if the relationship continued.

"My lover was furious when he heard. He felt he should be judged by his political effectiveness, not as a lover or husband. He tried very hard to persuade the aide otherwise but it was no use. My lover dug in his heels and insisted that we start going out much more together. From now on he wouldn't hide at all. It shattered me. I tried very hard for his sake, but I was always aware of people looking at me, the whispers, the pointed fingers.

"I started getting phone calls—people accusing me of being all sorts of things. Mostly the accusers were women, and they didn't sound young. Once, when I was walking along the street, a woman who worked in the party office came up to me and started shouting abuse. She must have felt very strongly or she wouldn't have chosen such a public place. Normally she was a mild-mannered woman but with me she acted a shrew. I ran away from her in tears.

"That was it, I decided. I couldn't go on with this. I couldn't hope to continue a relationship with such violent opposition from all sides. My lover tried to stop me, but I had had a year of unhappiness and that was no way to sustain a relationship. We'd begun to bicker over small things, and this was just our way of showing the strain we felt. I had to get away, so I got a job in a town about fifty miles away.

"I had six weeks alone before my lover started visiting me. We were still in his constituency and should have known that his presence in the town would not go unnoticed. The phone calls began again so I had the phone taken out. Then came the letters—all signed, so no one was worried about keeping their identities secret. They convinced me that I was fighting a force beyond me.

"I moved right away. I'm still in love with my lover and we have met twice in the last year. He's been shaken by it, too, but we're better off not seeing each other until we can decide what he wants to do. He believes he should get a divorce but he's very attached to his children and doesn't want to lose them. His wife has told him that she won't let him see them again if he pursues the idea of divorce.

"What makes me feel so bad is that I am unable to help him. I should be by his side, supporting him. But I haven't the courage. I've been branded by society for falling in love, and I can't face up to the continual accusations. With any luck his career won't suffer and perhaps if he gets through the next election, he'll be confident enough to go ahead with divorce. I suppose then it will all come out again about us, but by that time my wounds might have healed and I'll be strong enough to cope."

The mistress, like the stepmother, the mother-in-law, the witch and a host of other threatening female figures, has been stereotyped in our culture and mythologized in literature as a malevolent, dangerous woman. Clearly the realities of today's mistresses belie the image of the mistress as the temptress, the seducer of innocent victims, a cold, calculating woman who steals responsible men from the family hearth and breaks up marriages with abandon—in short, the Scarlet Woman, described in Revelation by St. John, who saw a vision of a woman "arrayed in purple and scarlet color" sitting upon a scarlet-colored beast. Upon her head were written the words "Babylon the Great, the mother of Harlots and abominations of the Earth."

These stereotypes and myths, which represent man's archetypal fear of succumbing to the destructive forces of his desire, are based upon an unconcealed double standard. There is one code of ethics for the mistress, another for a married man. Thus the mistress is judged, and judged harshly, while the married man is forgiven on the grounds that he was led astray. Since the very word "mistress" assumes a double standard, only an adulterous woman is thus labeled to describe her "crime." The adulterous man is simply described as a lover.

What emerges, then, from a study of the mistress today is the sexism implicit in our notion of fidelity and the Christian concept of adultery. Man the adulterer is spared the ignominy of labels, the burden of guilt. These are reserved, unless a man is an eminent public figure, for the female adulterer, who becomes the scapegoat for public hostility. She is the one who can never escape the social responsibility for the "crime" that she and her lover jointly commit in an illicit relationship.

"I do feel terrible guilt about it, but as with religion, you push the guilt to the back of your mind. You close your mind to it because you know you're getting what you need at the time."

Whether they like it or not, the majority of mistresses have to pretend they don't exist. They have to accept that their lovers deny their existence, at least to wives and colleagues, if not to close male friends. They have to accept that they must be hidden away from their lovers' worlds, that their meetings must be clandestine, that their feelings must not be demonstrated in public.

"You become furtive and paranoid about meeting. My heart used to race whenever I was going to see him. Then I realized it was fear that we might be seen, that someone would tell his wife he was having an affair. I knew too that my friends would be scornful of me for having anything to do with a married man."

Society might choose to mythologize the mistress in retrospect, but while she is alive and well and threatening, she simply does not exist. In her role as mistress she is "persona non grata"—an isolated woman living on the fringe of society, neither recognized nor integrated into it.

"Society knows we exist. They know we're here, but people don't like to admit it. Obviously the very fact that

we exist in such large numbers means we are, like the prostitute, filling a tremendous need. That in itself justifies our existence."

Women are often the severest critics of the mistress—understandably, for she represents a very real threat, particularly to women who are insecure about their own marriages. A mistress who is discovered often has projected onto her, as a consequence, the fears and anxieties of an entire community of wives. She may find herself, like Joan Gardner, transformed in the public mind into the treacherous, ruthless stereotype of the scarlet woman, while in reality she is probably vulnerable, confused, and insecure.

The exaggerated condemnation of the mistress also reflects the freemasonry of married people and the essentially hypocritical attitude prevalent in society today: that it doesn't matter how much a single person is hurt as long as nothing is allowed to endanger the married state. The feelings of most mistresses are consequently rarely considered by married couples—and particularly by the sorority of wives.

Wifely fears and anxieties that their husbands might secretly have a mistress are often compounded by feelings of envy. Part of the mystique of the mistress is that she is supposed to represent everything many wives feel they lack—glamor, freedom and irresponsibility. Standing over her sink in the morning, many a housewife, particularly the taken-for-granted-wife, must secretly fantasize a glamorous relationship (such as she imagines every mistress must have) where she is free from all responsibilities, loved and desired as a sexual partner. If she perceives herself, by contrast, as a distinctly unglamorous domestic appendage, she will understandably feel resentful, all too ready to focus this resentment on a "discovered" mistress—particularly a mistress who is discovered to be having an affair with her own spouse.

"Hell hath no fury like a woman scorned." Some wives, supported by the sorority, seem to feel that any action against, or slander of, the mistress is entirely justifiable when motivated by her "love" of her husband. Like Joan Gardner, whose lover's wife publicly slandered her, six mistresses commented on the vengeful treatment they had received from their lovers' wives.

"*His wife used to phone me all the time, at first just to abuse him, but when that failed to destroy our relationship, she started to tell lies. The first time I believed her. She told me he had come around after a business trip with all his things and promised to move back home again, when in fact she hadn't set eyes on him. When he finally moved in with me (or I thought it was finally—it lasted only a month) she would ring up every night about midnight and scream and cry and try to blackmail him—often within earshot of their children—telling him she was going to take tranquilizers and kill herself.*"

Another mistress, whose affair ended after eleven months of living with her lover, explained:

"*His wife's resentment played a great part in the misery of our lives together. She wanted to make us as unhappy as possible, not only by holding the divorce over our heads, but also by calling me a husband stealer and a hussy. Nothing would convince her that he was attracted to me. She was very cruel to me at times. For example, she once turned up at our apartment and gave me a lecture in front of a friend of hers, hurling abuse at me for over an hour and refusing to leave the apartment because she said it belonged to her husband. Her marriage had been bad, they had had fight after fight, she being as temperamental as he. Before I ever got involved with him she used to moan to me about him, and she enjoyed cutting him down in front of other people. Her biggest threat was that she would write to the newspapers (he was something of a public figure) and let everybody know. I always felt guilty about her, and in the end there was no one to blame but myself. I had decided to start the affair and keep it going; I was deceiving her. Yet it would have been someone else if it hadn't been me. I think he took a certain pride in showing me off—he wanted to prove something to her— perhaps because she had undermined him so much."*

Many mistresses, on the other hand, distorted and maligned the wives as much as they insisted the wives maligned them. A wife's reaction to another woman threatening her marriage is likely to be (understandably) violent and irrational. By condemning her for her irrational behavior, some mistresses were helping themselves alleviate their own guilt, in the same way that the wife, by condemning the mistress, alleviates her own resentment— a classic example of woman pitched against woman, fighting each other in a life-and-death struggle to "get" a man.

In one instance, however, the opposite happened. The mistress and the wife got together and not only discovered they had much in common but also that they liked each other enormously. Their exchanges were therefore supportive rather than recriminatory. This was, unfortunately, the exception that proved the rule. Indeed, two mistresses, active feminists themselves, found themselves condemned even by their feminist "sisters" for their affairs. One of these women, who had the utmost difficulty justifying her behavior, explained her dilemma:

> "I've rejected marriage as hypocritical and unworkable, yet I still find myself being judged and judging myself by these selfsame monogamous values. I find myself feeling enormously guilty for being the 'other woman' caught in the old syndrome of female rivalry. I tried initially to relate to his wife as a 'sister,' but she insists on referring to me before her children and others as the woman who took their father away from her. It is extremely difficult. I tried talking to her, but it's hopeless. I also tried to talk over my ambivalent feelings in a consciousness-raising group, but even there I felt myself being subtly condemned for my position."

The mistress, like the prostitute, fits uneasily into the feminist perspective. Sympathy might be extended retrospectively to feminist figures like George Eliot (Marianne Evans), whose twenty-five-year illicit relationship with Henry Lewis exiled her from society and precluded her burial in Westminster Abbey, or to feminist heroines like Anaïs Nin, whose affair with Django Reinhart is chronicled in *The Four Chambered Heart*. But as a category of woman she remains suspect.

Thus the mistress remains condemned on all sides—by wives, by society, and, most of all, by herself.

A wife, because of her relationship with her husband, has financial security, social acceptance, status and general approval, while the mistress, because of her relationship with the same man, has none of these vicariously gained advantages. Ironically, she is robbed of dignity and position because she is a "free" woman having a relationship with an "unfree" man.

The Marriage Maker: Fulfilling the Male Need (1)

Edna Reed has long auburn hair, a youthful, swinging gait, and looks as wholesome as the girl next door. She works in a small business firm and gives the appearance of being thoroughly contented with her lot in life.

"At the beginning of our relationship I was young enough to think I had been the cause of his marriage break-up. But when the crisis was over and he went back to his wife, the feelings we had for each other for the next seven years kept his marriage going.

"I was twenty-five when I met him. We worked together and we both realized that there was an enormous attraction. I was engaged at the time, but it wasn't till after I was married that the affair started. I wanted to be equal, you see; he was married, so I had to be married too. I had no intention of attacking or trying to oust his wife and the two children.

"My husband and I saw each other only on weekends because he was attending school in another city, and my lover's family lived far enough outside the city for him to be able to find reasons why he couldn't get back at night. We had plenty of freedom. At first we stayed in hotels, then we rented an apartment, which he wouldn't let me pay for. It was separate from both our ways of life, a place for our meetings. We were in love and we knew we had to maintain double lives to stay in love.

"Then without consulting me he told his wife he wanted to leave her. I was really furious with him. I knew I wasn't stealing from her and it seemed to me essential that he be dishonest with her to save her suffering. But no, he went and told her. I was angry because he should have had more foresight. He deserved the way his wife reacted. Her pride was hurt. She was determined to get her revenge and the best way was through the children, because my lover was a devoted father. She told one of the twins, the one he particularly cared about, that Daddy didn't love him anymore. His son started having nightmares and everyone was very worried about him. My lover saw this son as a replica of himself and when he responded the way he did, he felt under attack.

"My lover felt he had to do what he said he'd do and he left home, but after three months he went back. I'd stopped seeing him from the moment he told his wife. I decided to leave my job and go work nearer my husband. I had the best intentions of making our marriage work, but I couldn't get my lover out of my mind. I was having hallucinations, seeing him everywhere. I would rush up to someone I thought was he, but the face would turn into a stranger's.

"At this point we made contact again, and for eighteen months we met once, twice a month. During this time we realized just how deep our relationship was. Our most important realization was that there were two strands to both our lives and it would be a terrible mistake to get them intertwined. Our double lives continued even more scrupulously after that.

"When my father first learned about the affair, I

remember him saying: 'Don't hurt other people and keep your tongue in your head.' I thought he was being cynical, but he was right . . . it is important not to hurt other people.

"I think being a mistress is the worst of both worlds. It takes a certain type of personality to always play a double role and not go round the bend. I'm sure this is why most people settle in the end for what they've got, rather than pursue something that only gives joy occasionally. I know one thing—if we had ever married it would have been essential for us both to have been faithful because we both knew just how capable we were at lying. Having to continually hide things was a shattering experience.

"But it was an enlightening and enlarging experience knowing my lover. I'd been to a school for young ladies and my background was very narrow. It was like coming out of a tunnel into the light. And I learned something about myself I hadn't known before—what turns me on most about a man is kindness. My lover was not only kind to me but he was also kind to his wife and children after that first bad error.

"Actually it was his kindness that gave me the worst hurt in those seven years. It was the one time he was unfaithful—with a whore he'd given a lift after they'd left the same bar. She'd invited him in and he felt it good manners to accept. He made love to her just as he did to his wife—because it was good manners to. I was upset because I felt he didn't owe her anything. But he used sex as a language. He used to say, 'If it were demanded of me socially, I would make love to a gorilla.'

"When we eventually started to break up I wanted him to make love to me more often, because this brought us closer together mentally. By this time my own marriage had finished but the reasons for that went back to long before the marriage, to two children being unable to grow up. We had nothing in common and it took marriage to prove it to us.

"Then I met a man who asked me to live with him. I was tired of living life alone, of only seeing my lover when he could get away from his responsibilities. This man needed me, he made me feel wanted. He was very kind to me and I realized I wanted to let this man give to me. I felt I was the one who was always giving, first to my husband who wanted a mother, then to my lover who was using me as a means of keeping his marriage together. I liked the change.

"I went to live with him and for the first few months I went on seeing my lover, though we both knew our relationship couldn't last much longer. We'd changed jobs so we weren't in the same office. We just ran out of steam. But it took a long time to end. We kept avoiding the decision because sex was good to the end. When it came I was really quite emotionally affected. I never thought I would be, but I felt sad that this passion would no longer be in my life.

"Just before we broke up he gave me a fur coat. It was a joke, a thing to do with mistresses. He said he wanted to make love to me while I was wearing it. And of course we did. When we split up I put the coat in my wardrobe and it was several years before the emotion connected with it had died enough for me to wear it.

"I was very angry when I heard a year after we'd broken up that he was in the divorce courts. His wife got the divorce, and it wasn't on grounds of adultery. There was no other woman involved, the marriage just came to an end. I think the relationship I had with him kept the marriage going all those years. He was a better husband

and father as a result. He went home happy, he had better understanding of others' feelings. I can only imagine what he must have been like in that last year without a relationship to sustain him. He needed more than a wife and family, and as he was a selfish man he must have made his feelings known. If he'd started another deep relationship, his marriage might still be going today."

Although the mistress is still popularly assumed to be a prime cause of marriage break-up, it is in fact highly probable that she maintains far more marriages than she destroys. Certainly our research bore out the fact that a mistress who fulfills the unmet needs of a marriage, thereby masking its deficiencies, may serve to prop up and perpetuate a marriage for a long period of time. She may even, by providing a release for the husband's fantasies and perhaps indirectly increasing his tolerance for his wife, turn a tottering marriage into a very good one, as had happened with one of the men we interviewed:

"After twenty-five years of gazing at my wife over the breakfast table I had begun to use her as a scapegoat for all my many dissatisfactions with my life. I thought half my problems stemmed from the fact that I was saddled with this woman, and I had continual fantasies about running off with other women. When I finally found myself deeply involved with a woman who turned out to be very shallow and manipulating, it made me realize what a strong and good person my wife was, and I developed a whole new feeling of respect and affection for her."

The Marriage Maker: Fulfilling the Male Need (1)

Edna Reed, in contrast, compensated for the gaps in her lover's marriage to such an extent that the marriage collapsed when their affair ended. Three-fourths of the women in our sample were obviously playing a marriage-making role, although they varied a great deal in their recognition of it. Twelve women were convinced that a man who was getting satisfaction from an extra-marital affair would return to his wife a happier and presumably better husband (discounting the alternative possibility that he might return home more acutely aware of his marriage's deficiencies and become even more dissatisfied).

"His wife was too busy with her own life and the children's to ask him very often how he was. I was always there to listen, to boost him up when he felt down. He never left my apartment without a smile on his face."

Another woman, whose affair had lasted for eleven years, commented:

"I know my lover is a happier husband because of our affair. One side of him is only satisfied through his marriage—I satisfy the other side. Before me, there was a great void in his life. He had prolonged depressions and went on drinking binges. He hasn't had one of these since our affair began."

Four mistresses, on the other hand, would undoubtedly have been horrified to realize they were playing a marriage-making role, since they hoped to become wives themselves. By showing that they were better partners, they hoped their lovers would decide to abandon their deficient marriages and seek a permanent, legal relationship with them. Two women in particular, whose relationships had lasted three and five years respectively, were proud of the way they were able to put aside their own problems, listen to their lovers' complaints about work, and generally boost their egos. What they failed to see was that the deficiencies of their lovers' marriages were, as a consequence, at least temporarily covered up.

Once they realized this, there would undoubtedly be a crisis, and the delicate balance of their lovers' lives would be shattered. The result might possibly be the collapse of their marriages.

It is hardly surprising that married mistresses seemed to be the most successful marriage-makers—sometimes for their own marriages. Two married mistresses in our study had decided that they preferred to continue both their marriages and their affairs.

"The sexual and emotional rapport found in an affair can be a threat to a marriage. You tend to reappraise your marriage and spotlight the parts that have broken down. But if you feel your marriage is worth continuing despite the areas of incompatibility, you may find that an affair releases sublimated feelings which, when they rise to the surface, hold the marriage together. That is what happened to me."

The other married mistress also felt that her marriage had been strengthened by the affair:

"I'm a happier person and a better sexual partner to my husband. Before I had an affair, our bedtime life had become terribly stolid and boring. Being with someone else and doing different things means I'm bringing home different ideas, so sex with my husband has become far more interesting."

In the case of Edna Reed, it seems that the affair prolonged her own marriage as well: she was able to tolerate the deficiencies of her marriage while the affair was in progress, and the break-up of her marriage coincided with the end of the affair. And although she was ambivalent about her lover's being married—she complained about his "using" her to keep his marriage together—she obviously did not want to break the marriage up, since she refused to see him while he was separated from his wife.

Another married mistress maintained she would lie if necessary to prevent her husband or lover's wife from finding out about the relationship:

"Denying it will keep both our marriages together, which is the main thing as far as I'm concerned. His wife is such an inoffensive person and a good wife and mother. So is my husband, whom I am still very fond of. Why should they be hurt because of us?"

Several mistresses were very wary of the idea of breaking up a marriage simply because they didn't feel they could face the problems that would result, especially where children were involved.

"If it got to the stage where it was a case of ending the marriage I would finish with him. I love him so much that I wouldn't destroy him. His kids are very important to him. I would like to marry him and have a child by him, but I would have to break the marriage up, and that I couldn't do."

Two mistresses made conscious decisions never to bring up the subject of her lover's leaving his wife. One explanation was valid for both:

"*I kept thinking of what would happen to the children. I am a child of a broken marriage and I know how much it hurt me.*"

One simply saw more advantages to her present position:

"*I prefer to be a mistress. I wouldn't marry my lover even if he left his wife. I prefer being the other woman— it's a more exciting caviar relationship. You're not taken for granted as you are when you become a wife.*"

Another woman who had no desire to break up her lover's marriage summed up her role:

"*A mistress fills her lover's need to talk as much as his sexual needs. Until he met me, my lover had never really talked to a woman. I played a part in his life that a wife couldn't. As we both wanted a little bit of life that wasn't respectable, we were happy.*"

The fact that a man, relating simultaneously to a wife and a mistress, can express different sides of himself and satisfy very different needs in each relationship explains how it is sometimes possible for a man to continue an affair and a marriage simultaneously for a long period, with each relationship apparently supporting and complementing the other.

The Marriage Maker: Fulfilling the Male Need (2)

Paul Gendel is a thin, balding, fifty-ish department-store manager. His protruding nose prevents him from being "handsome," but he does have a certain panache and old-world charm which more than compensate for his physical flaws.

"When I look back on my life I realize that I've had an affair for every year I've been alive. I'm fifty now . . . but the affairs of course didn't just last a year. Some were much shorter, and there were only really three that I'd call long-term, ones that had major effects on me.

"My present wife, whom I married two years ago, was my mistress for twenty-five years. She was, I suppose, the reason for my first marriage breaking up. Once my first wife knew about her, she withdrew from the marriage, so I moved out and in with my mistress.

"My second-longest relationship lasted twenty years. We were very fond of each other, and if the circumstances had been right at the time I might have married her. She was the wife of one of my friends and he left her stranded with three kids. I used to see her at least once a week because she lived near to one of my business interests. I began to support her financially and it grew from that.

"The third affair is major in a different way. And it was an unfortunate experience, because it convinced me that there are a lot of women around who will try and break up a marriage, if they think they'll get something out of it. In this case I'd formed the relationship and she was pregnant before I realized what she was all about. I'd got involved with her for all the wrong reasons . . . she was a convenience that suited my life at that stage. She went ahead and had the child: it was blackmail of the worst kind. I think I hated her for doing it because I felt it was disgusting to bring a third person into the situation where there could be no love or security. I hated her, I hated myself, I hated everything about the situation. It gave me a scare, I can tell you.

"My life might not be as it is, and my attitude to women might have been different if I'd had children through either of my marriages. I most probably would have considered myself selfish in having affairs because those could have put the children's futures at risk. Children would have taken the need for affairs away because they require emotional as well as physical energy. I'd have had little left over for anything else.

"I accepted that I was a person who needed other relationships. I think a prerequisite is being free from guilt—anyone who believes in monogamy and fidelity should not even bother pursuing other women because they won't enjoy them when they get them.

"I never sleep with a woman unless I'm very fond of her and attracted to her: just going to bed with someone I met would be prostitution.

"Most of the women I've had affairs with I've met through my business associations—secretaries, customers, supervisors. Some women I would see only once a month, others once a week. I've owned several apartments through the years, and at one time I shared with another man who had a similar temperament and similar interests in pursuit,

The Marriage Maker: Fulfilling the Male Need (2)

so I met my women at these apartments or at their own.

"All my affairs have been sexual, though on occasions there's been much more to them than sex. I've always been excessively fond of women and I've always found them much more interesting to be with than men. It's no effort for me to be interested in them as people—but it could be that this is an excuse for my immaturity. I've never felt I've treated women as sexual objects or that I've used them.

"I never expect a woman to be faithful to me. If I found out that my second wife were involved with someone, I'd just say, 'Good luck to you.' I am truly not possessive in this way. As I know how self-indulgent I am, it would not be possible for me to have a double standard.

"Just one thing about women disappoints me. All of them—and this cuts across social and intellectual barriers—want in the end to be kept or married. My wife is a very intelligent and a very independent woman, and when it came to the crunch she too wanted to be a wife, to be kept and cared for.

"None of my affairs have been a threat to my present marriage, or even a threat to the relationship I had before we married . . . but they have certainly added spice and incentive to life.

"I might be fooling myself, but I believe I could have been faithful if I'd been required to. I mean, anybody could put up with one person all his life just as you can put up with all sorts of things. You could put up with living on bread and cheese all your life but you'd miss out on a lot. I believe in living life to the full. I'm well off so I don't see the point of acting half-dead. I've always enjoyed myself and have never believed in the stoical, puritanical tradition.

"Every so often I wonder whether the women I get involved with, or indeed any woman who has an affair, can get anything satisfactory out of it. A relationship consists more than anything of stolen moments, so why should women bother? I suppose it must partly be the challenge. Few women will ever accept that you can be happily married and yet have affairs."

Both the long-standing, exclusive extra-marital relationship and the string of successive affairs often stem from unsatisfied, sometimes unconscious, needs in the married man.

Many mistresses described themselves as "putty filling the cracks of a marriage," and most lovers similarly "blamed" their extra-marital involvement on their marriages which, they explained, had failed to fulfill all (in some cases, any) of their needs. The most obvious reason for a man to seek a relationship outside his marriage is disappointment with his wife—especially if she has been expected to fulfill all his deepest needs. Although it is now widely accepted that one person cannot be expected to satisfy all the needs and desires of another, the myth endures.

"To be honest I found it glamorous to have a mistress, and the fact that I felt it was illegal and wrong added to the excitement. But she was an emotional foil too. She would listen to me all evening. Not like my wife, who was so filled with her own problems that she wouldn't listen to me at all. My mistress was always considerate and put me first."

Six of the men we interviewed complained explicitly of wives who didn't boost their egos, or make them feel important or attractive. Some men, on the surface at least, seemed to want nothing more than a glamorous younger woman to flatter their self-images. Several felt they had simply "grown apart" from their wives to such an extent that they both had entirely different needs and desires:

"For several years before I met my mistress I found myself drifting away from my wife. I became more and more attracted to other women and flirted madly, at first for the excitement of it, I suppose; but after a while I began to realize that I was particularly attracted to women who were the opposite of my wife. Slowly, especially in my present affair, it dawned on me that I was depending on these women to supply all the things I wasn't getting in my marriage. Only through them could I make my marriage survive."

Another man put it more bluntly:

"If I didn't have affairs I couldn't stay in my marriage. I just can't stay at home. Other women keep my marriage together."

Another man explained:

"I like my wife. She's a nice person, but I don't love her in the sense of lusting after her. I'm not on the same wavelength she is. Ten minutes of conversation and that's it. We have very little in common. She's a good woman, a marvelous wife and mother, but she's just not my sort. It's a failure, but because of the children, I don't want to break up my marriage."

In a marriage where a man and a wife relate almost exclusively as "Mom and Dad," a mistress will often fulfill her lover's desire to be treated as more than merely "Dad."

One man complained:

"In my marriage, I am the fix-it man, the breadwinner, the teacher, the disciplinarian. I am a series of roles and functions, which I wouldn't resent so much if I were only allowed to be myself as well."

The most easily recognizable and frequently mentioned "unfulfilled need" or lack in a marriage was, of course, sex. One man, for example, who had had his first extra-marital affair after eleven years of perfunctory and unsatisfactory sex with his wife, had become so addicted to it that he had been involved ever since in a compulsive, non-stop string of affairs. The marriage endures, but he is unable to live any longer, he says, without continual sexual gratification from a variety of partners.

Another man in the same situation concluded:

"If a man is loving by nature and loves sex, there is only one thing for him to do: get a mistress where he is one thing and one thing only—a lover."

Normally, however, sexual deprivation is only the tip of the iceberg. In fact a man is seeking (consciously or unconsciously) in his extra-marital relationship gratification of a whole series of needs, which will vary according to the state of his marriage.

Several mistresses realized that their liaisons with their lovers were either started or given impetus by a strain in the marriage.

The Marriage Maker: Fulfilling the Male Need (2)

"In seven years I have learned little about the substance of the relationship he has with his wife. I think it's a good marriage but she's the stronger partner. She's in control. I think I turned up at some point of crisis. That's passed but I'm still around. Their relationship has changed but it's not been ruined."

Pregnancy is a particular stress-point in marriage, and three mistresses realized in retrospect that the intensity of their relationships with their lovers increased during these times.

Often the reasons for an affair, although they may be projected onto a marriage partner, stem from a deeper, instinctual source, related as much to factors such as a man's "life phase" (the notorious "male menopause") as to his actual marriage situation.

The majority of men in our sample were heading for their fortieth birthdays or were well beyond them and seemed to regard this fact with a considerable degree of anxiety. Traditionally, the years after forty were regarded as a plateau sloping gradually to old age and retirement, the purpose of this second half of life being a slow divorce from sexuality and preparation to die content. Today, however, more men seem to be rising up in protest against the idea of "rest and retirement." Indeed, its imminence alone is often enough to provoke a personal crisis in a man's life—a frantic desire to stave off middle age and to prove to himself that he still has a 'second chance' in life (if not a second adolescence). And what better way to do it than to have an affair.

"For the last seven years I had been getting very restless. We were both increasingly automatic in our responses to each other. We had nothing warm or vital *about us. I felt as though she had moved out of a central room in myself and left it empty. My life was sickeningly routine. I would definitely say that if I wasn't actually looking, I was ready for an affair for several years before I actually had one."*

A man suffering from this sense of inchoate, unfocused depression is ripe for an affair. A woman through whom he perceives he will be able to revitalize his life will doubtless constitute an irresistible attraction.

But resorting to an extra-marital affair to fill in the gaps in one's life can have serious disadvantages—for the man as well as the woman—unless the mistress and her lover expect the same from the relationship. Where the relationship proceeds according to a definite set of rules, tacitly agreed upon by both mistress and lover, it is possible for the situation to endure for a long time. This is the exception, however, because most mistresses regard their position as that of second best. The resultant dissatisfaction often breeds guilt and bitterness—on both sides.

The Male Conflict

Alan Frost is a small, dapper man of about thirty-five with closely cropped hair and an earnest, sincere demeanor. He works as an editor at a large publishing house.

"When I first became involved in an affair, I think I had subconsciously decided that although I believed myself in love with my wife, it wasn't enough. I needed more. So I was on the lookout for another woman and I found her in the office—she was my secretary.

"The affair began slowly at first, but after the first six months or so we developed the most enormous passion for each other. For a year it was all ego support and passion and roses. But then suddenly, when she began to put pressure on me to leave my wife, it all began to collapse. Initially I had felt very much in love with her, but as soon as I realized she wanted more from the relationship than I was prepared to give, I shut off my feelings for her.

"I was very dishonest about it. I knew in my heart, when she began putting pressure on me—when would I leave my wife? when could we get an apartment together? —that I never would, but for some reason I just couldn't tell her. I made up all sorts of elaborate excuses and was, I have to admit now, really dishonest to her, a real son-of-a-bitch. I didn't want the affair to stop. I wanted the love and ego support and attention, but at the same time I wanted absolutely *no* responsibility.

"Somehow I had planned in my mind what I wanted from her. The usual selfish thing where you just want something *your* way—nasty, but not untypical. To all intents and purposes I had a good marriage. I had a wife who trusted me, which of course makes a man feel very guilty when he's unfaithful. We were doing very nest-like things, like buying a house, getting mortgages and so on. So I just kept on making excuses and even got to the stage where I began to tell my mistress I wasn't sure of *her* feelings, which was a particularly vicious way of evading responsibility.

"I knew the affair had to end, but I wanted to draw it out as long as possible, and I had rationalized this basically egotistical desire by saying that I had a responsibility to withdraw as gently as possible from the affair. I couldn't just say, That's it, push off. I felt I owed her some explanation for why I wouldn't end my marriage. Ultimately this was much worse, of course, because I gave her an explanation which asked her to blame herself, and enabled me to escape the truth. And I did evade the truth for quite a while. It was only after it was all over that the truth about the whole thing finally hit home.

"It ended when she realized at last that I wasn't going to do anything. Finally she just took off overseas, and I didn't see her for a few years. One day, when I had finally faced up to what I had done, I felt a responsibility to establish some sort of truth, so we had lunch and I said, o.k. here's what I think motivated me. I got it off my chest and it made me feel a bit better. Not much better, mind you, because ironically, in the process of being dishonest to her and with myself, and evasive and cowardly, I came to despise myself. Instead of getting the ego-reinforcement which was what I really wanted from the affair, I began to hate myself, and it eroded my ego even further. It taught me a lot. All along, some corner of myself was aware whenever I wasn't being honest with myself, and yet I seemed incapable of acting in any other way. It became an unavoidable pattern. But what I eventually learned was what a miserable way it is to conduct a life, to build it on a tissue of lies and deceptions. It's very self-destructive and ultimately self-defeating. I learned not to want to do it again—the experience was so excruciating and debilitating and I became so disgusted with myself.

"A lot of men who have affairs go on living in a sort of fantasy-deception world all their lives. I guess they either just block out that part of them which despises what they're doing, or somehow they just aren't aware of it, or perhaps they decide they just don't care anyway. My affair led me to a much greater self-awareness and growth, but others just reconcile themselves to whatever negative consequences they experience from their double life in terms of pain, suffering, guilt and other emotions that seem to be produced by an affair. They just accept it as the price they must pay, almost as a punishment, I guess.

"I used to see her every day in the office of course, and after work we would go to her nearby apartment for a few hours. Then, every night, I had to go home, and I never wanted to. According to what I was trying to prove to myself, I would do one of a number of things when I got back to my wife. Sometimes I would make love to her, which I thought was rather clever. It seemed to show that I could handle the whole situation—which of course was nonsense—and I always satisfied her, even though it was a bit exhausting for me. Sometimes I would feel like a little boy who comes back to his mother, having stolen some cookies from the cookie jar, and unable to tell her about it. Then there was the feeling that I had to be prepared for the chance that she was going to ask something she had never asked before. There always lurked the possibility that she had found out, so there was always some tension, a sort of let's-be-ready-to-confront-this feeling. Some additional tension, too, if I got home later than usual—then I had to lie. I suffered anxiety, guilt, fear, insecurity, though at the time I wasn't fully conscious of these underlying emotions.

"Now I realize that a good amount of my psychic energy was burned up with these negative and, I suppose, masochistic feelings. Especially in the last year, when my mistress was really putting pressure on me and I deliberately, masochistically kept myself in the affair, as though it would somehow salve my conscience. I told myself I was doing a "duty." But I was doing a terrible thing, and making it all much worse."

The mistress, as most men would have her, is a perfect fantasy. She is an ideal companion: sexually satisfying, emotionally gratifying, ego boosting, undemanding, full of sympathy, always glamorous, infinitely understanding—a cross between Florence Nightingale and Sophia Loren.

Perfect in fantasy—but imperfect in reality. For while the cloistered circumstances in which an affair normally develops—with its intensity, insecurity, secrecy and excitement—serve initially to nourish the fantasy, the ultimate reality is, with few exceptions, confusion, deception and anguish.

Some men, it is true, get pleasure from hovering on the edge of a precipice, without any intention of taking the jump. And a few, the lucky ones with endless money, travel opportunities, or preferably both, can enjoy the fantasy for a long time. One mistress involved with just such a fortunate gentleman described their relationship as a veritable fairy tale:

"We meet in luxury hotels all over the world. I found the way he lavished money on me embarrassing at first because I wasn't used to it. I am now. We go out to the best and most expensive places, have lavish food, vintage wine—everything. We've only met in the same country twice. He rings me and says 'Come to Geneva for the night, or Hong Kong for the week.' It's been fantastic for me. I've got the excitement most women dream of but never have."

Glamor, weekends in the Bahamas and other exotic places, uninhibited sex . . . for the vast majority of men, daily commuters from unexotic suburbia, such a fantasy is fed only by its unattainability. Practical exigencies—the nine-to-five work schedule, a joint bank account—preclude all but a harmless flirtation with it. For, as one man ruefully observed, to be enduringly successful with a mistress, a man needs a great deal of unaccountable time on his hands, considerable money, a guilt-free conscience, an ability to lie effortlessly, and a capacity to live an almost schizophrenic existence.

One man, a life-long pursuer of extra-marital adventures, attributed the considerable success of his affairs more to his economic status than to any personal attribute.

"I'm convinced that having affairs is an upper-middle-class (in the economic sense of the word) pleasure, a luxury item in a man's life that few can afford. A man who not only can provide his wife with a good standard of living but who also has extensive business interests is in

the best position. You must be your own boss, have a business that demands your time in the evenings and on weekends. Most women will accept this as an excuse so long as they can reap the financial rewards. I think I would have given up long ago if I'd had the mess and complications of a nine-to-fiver. It would be impossible. You would have to make excuses not only to your wife but also to your employer. I wouldn't have had the capacity to work it out."

Even those not excluded by economic insufficiency or other insurmountable practical obstacles frequently bring into a relationship, in the impossible fantasy expectations they project onto their mistresses, the seeds of its ultimate dissolution. Fairly typical, it seems, is the man who seeks in his mistress things he cannot find in his wife—a woman who responds to a different set of needs altogether, and whom he does not expect to share the same wifely demands, the same need for security, and so on. It comes as a rude and unwelcome shock, therefore, when the mistress begins to act in a manner uncomfortably resembling his wife. Ultimately seeking to find himself, not another woman, he projects his disappointments onto his mistress, who, not living up to his unrealistic fantasy, makes him feel disappointed, even cheated.

Thus, Alan Frost began to switch off his feelings the moment "wifely" pressure began to be exerted. Another lover, who confessed he had been "wrong to expect that my mistress would play just the role I wanted her to play—I never really gave a thought to her needs," explained how confused and irritated he felt when his glamorous fantasy began to reveal her real, vulnerable, emotional needs.

"For the first six months of our affair we didn't mention my wife or family at all. We just went out madly, had a wild sex life and developed a great intellectual rapport. I was ecstatic. It was a time of excitement, expanding horizons, a feeling of upsurge and growth after a long period of stasis. Then one night when I arrived an hour and a half late for dinner, she broke down and said, in essence, 'I just can't go on like this—either live with me or leave.' I was paralyzed and terrified. I was forced to confront the reality of what I had been doing—blithely getting myself into a terrible trap from which there was no apparent escape. Our whole relationship changed overnight."

A man in such a situation is indeed in a dilemma. One part of him is intensely dependent on the love, sexuality, ego-reinforcement of his mistress, and would like to throw away everything else for these. Another part of him is appalled by his infidelity and the new set of responsibilities and obligations he has brought upon himself, and wants to escape from the whole mess and retreat back into the security and stability of the domestic hearth. Still another part of him is guilt-ridden, confused, possibly even—as happened to Alan Frost—disgusted with himself for the lies he is continually telling one woman in order to see the other, for the deceptions and dishonesty of the double life.

Those who don't eventually abandon the effort and break off the affair often linger in this limbo world of torment and indecision indefinitely, pulled in two directions at once, trying to respond adequately to two sets of demands, two sets of responsibilities, two women (and possibly children) needing attention and reassurance. Torn between love for his mistress and responsibility toward his family, between the seductiveness of a whole new life and the comfortable status quo, many men become completely immobilized.

One man, having insisted to his mistress that his marriage was in ruins and that he simply could not live without her, spent four years vacillating between mistress and wife, lurching from crisis to crisis, ultimatum to ultimatum. When the two women finally got together after all the promises and prevarications, they discovered that he had managed all these years to successfully persuade the wife that he had no intention of leaving home and was definitely going to end the affair, while convincing his mistress that he was going to leave his wife and move in with her. Had his mistress not eventually given up in despair, her trust in him eroded by the continual dissembling, he might have lingered on in this state of indecision indefinitely.

Such a man, wracked by indecision, finds that his ephemeral ecstasy has given way to agony. He will probably wonder at this stage whether the initial ecstasy was worth the prolonged confusion and uncertainty that is so often its price.

One man in such a dilemma insisted:

"Most men, if they sat down and thought seriously about it, would probably decide that having a mistress, as opposed to having a casual affair, just isn't worth the trouble and effort involved."

While some will take comfort in the sentiment expressed by Bertrand Russell: "I have sought love because it brings ecstasy—ecstasy so great that I would have sacrificed all the rest of my life for a few hours of this joy," others will silently wish they had sacrificed their few hours of joy for a lifetime of peace. And while some, like Alan Frost, will learn and evolve and grow from the experience, however painful, others will apparently gain nothing from it, but continue moving blindly from affair to affair in an endless pattern of evasion and escape.

The Marriage Breaker

John Roper is a short, middle-aged journalist with a nervous twitch in his right eye and a generally anxious, self-effacing manner. He often breaks off in the middle of a sentence, as though he had forgotten what he meant to say.

"I'm a very ordinary man who would have gone on being married forever if I hadn't been so besotted with a woman. I'd been married thirteen years when I met her and I was completely bowled over. We saw each other constantly for seven months, and when I realized how important she was to me I told my wife and asked for a divorce.

"But nothing happens as easily as that. It took a year for the situation to resolve itself. I felt so guilty about what I was doing to my wife and my children and about the responsibilities I was neglecting that I wanted to ease my conscience by trying to lessen the effect of my decision to leave. We'd had a good marriage till that point.

"My to-ing and fro-ing between my wife and my mistress caused distress to my mistress as well. She was convinced the marriage was terrible, and I think this salved her conscience. I once read an article on advice to second wives that began, 'Rule 1: Never assume that the first wife was a bitch.' I think that's absolutely right. My mistress couldn't believe it.

"My wife was understandably resentful about my

leaving her for another woman. She had reason to be upset; our children then were twelve and eight, the worst possible ages for their parents to break up. But I had no idea that her bitterness would make her so vengeful—she used the children as a form of blackmail and even now, eight years later, my children haven't accepted my mistress.

"I was leading a fairly typical upper-middle-class life before this happened, and there I was at the age of forty throwing it all over to go and live in an apartment in another city. It was a hell of a break.

"I'm sure very few men leave home because of the mistress though. It's much easier to continue the status quo, perhaps having a mistress on the side. Usually men can put up with even the worst marriages because they can survive by sublimating themselves in work or outside interests. The pattern a man builds up is comfortable, secure. He's not sure what he might get himself into if he broke up the marriage. At least by keeping the marriage going he has some control over tomorrow.

"I wasn't looking for a long-term affair when I met the woman who became my mistress. I saw it as temporary, but after three months I realized I was passionately in love, in a way I'd never been before. I was obsessed by her, and that's the only reason why my marriage broke up. I couldn't in all honesty continue a relationship with my wife knowing that I felt so much for another woman. It would have been too messy and complicated to keep a secret affair going. I'm not the sort of person who lies and dissembles with ease.

"With the wisdom of hindsight it's awfully difficult to say whether I did the right thing. Had I known the agony and pain of it beforehand I might not have done it. I just didn't know what I was letting myself in for.

"I still love my mistress, but I'm cynical about this true love that writers and others are always holding up as the pinnacle of experience between a man and a woman. I don't think there is such a thing. When my marriage broke up and I left I was definitely going to marry my mistress. We just had to wait till the divorce came through. It took six years before my wife got herself into a frame of mind where she could actually go into a court about a divorce. In that time of waiting my mistress became very bitter. In fact the whole period of disentanglement caused scars that haven't healed. She even today seethes with jealousy when I mention my wife or arrange to meet her and the children.

"Our years together have been very hard because we inherited the baggage of a broken marriage. All the guilt and resentment were transferred from one relationship to the other. We should have faced up to them. But we didn't and they have eroded our relationship.

"Perhaps it was because I was so obsessed by her that I didn't realize the incompatibilities between us. Every so often a little red flag would wave in my mind and I'd feel uncertain, wary, but I ignored all these warnings. I pushed them into the back of my mind believing that love would help us overcome and iron out all these difficulties.

"Living together brought out all the basic incompatibilities. She's a career woman and we compete with each other. All sorts of jealousies and problems crop up from this. The differences between us made it impossible for us to live together and now we have separate apartments. We still see a great deal of each other, but between us is a sort of love–hate. We can survive only by living apart.

"My wife was the exact opposite of my mistress. She had never worked and she made being a wife and mother a career. She was very good in the domestic sense; she was really somewhat of a *hausfrau*. My mistress is completely independent, and I can't say which of the two ways I like better. The problems with my mistress seem immense, and I can't see what will happen to us eventually. But we're still in love. At least we seem to need each other.

"I don't know whether we'll ever marry. What we imagined each other to be eight years ago has been proven false. I don't think we've yet found in each other what we're looking for. But if we had both faced up to those resentments instead of pushing them aside we might have had a happier relationship today."

The mistress who actually causes a marriage breakdown, as we have seen, is comparatively rare. While the existence of a mistress and her subsequent discovery might act as a catalyst in a marriage breakdown, she herself is rarely the reason for its failure. More typically, she is the symptom of an already established incompatibility.

Most of the mistresses we interviewed realized they were unlikely to break up a marriage, and this realization obviously assisted some of them in rationalizing their behavior and diminishing their feelings of guilt. When asked if they thought mistresses tended to break up marriages, the majority were categoric that they did not:

"No, I think if anything they tend to *keep them together*."

"It's the other way around. Men don't take mistresses unless they have a shaky marriage in the first place."

"The only time a mistress breaks up a marriage is

when the marriage is vulnerable. In other words, when it's rotten or dead."

Of the four mistresses we interviewed who had played a part in a marriage breakdown, none appeared to have played a decisive role, the seeds of marriage failure having been sown long before they entered their lovers' lives. The marriages of three men we interviewed had broken down, but only one man—John Roper—attributed this breakdown to the existence and discovery of a mistress.

All of which reinforces the opinion of many divorce lawyers, such as Neil Fleishman, author of the controversial *Counsel for the Damned*, who argue that adultery rarely plays a decisive role in contemporary divorce. Most divorces are initiated by women, Fleishman points out, and the fact remains that most wives are more likely to stick it out, often through repeated humiliations (and mistresses), unless the husband actually runs off with his mistress and deserts her. A wife discovering the existence of adultery "may grin or she may groan, but she will bear it," Mr. Fleishman insists. And indeed, in the six instances we learned of where wives had discovered their husbands' infidelity, divorce had not occurred.

Despite this, the conception of the dangerous, marriage-breaking mistress still holds the public imagination. Almost everyone has heard of some marriage which, rumor has it, collapsed because of the intervention of a "husband-stealing" mistress, for it is these cases that make the headlines. What is seldom appreciated is that these sensational stories are only the tip of the adultery iceberg, beneath which lies the reality of thousands of ordinary affairs which are conducted secretly throughout our society but which, because they do not cause the disruption of a marriage, never come to light.

Three women we interviewed did admit that they were trying to take their lovers away from their wives. Seven confessed to wishing or fantasizing a miraculous or painless ending to their lovers' marriage, and two said they nurtured a secret wish that their lovers' wives would suddenly die, run off with another man or somehow disappear from the scene. Needless to say, their wishes had not come true. For while many men similarly dream of quietly and abruptly disappearing with their mistresses, freeing themselves from the responsibilities and commitments of the marriage, few ultimately translate these dreams into reality.

The mistress whose lover does leave his wife may find herself playing the role of a safety net, giving a man the moral support and strength to take the initial leap, for few men are prepared to leave home without the reassuring arms of another woman.

"I doubt I would have left my wife if my mistress hadn't been there to go to; I'm basically a coward and I wouldn't have done anything about leaving. My mistress was the catalyst."

Usually, however, she has no control over whether or not she will be called upon to play a part in a marriage breakdown. For, with the exception of the bitter mistress who rings her lover's wife, or an interfering outsider who feels "duty bound" to inform about an affair, almost invariably the decision to tell or not to tell is left to the husband. A letter casually left in a pocket, a thoughtless remark that can only arouse suspicion—such things as these can precipitate a crisis. One husband explained how he had planned for months so that a letter would be found at the appropriate time. And while no others were as premeditated as this, most realized in retrospect that subconsciously they had wanted to be found out.

Even when a mistress does inadvertently precipitate the break-up, the break itself may be only short-lived.

"He stayed away for three months because he felt he had to make a stand, but he knew all along he had to go back to his wife and family. He couldn't bear the thought of his daughter, whom he really did love, turning against him. During that time, we saw each other only to talk. Our affair was over."

For a husband wrenched from the comforts and habitual security of the family home will not adjust easily, if at all, to a diminished standard of living, social pressure and a deprivation of his habitual environment.

"It's bloody miserable when you first separate, because the one who leaves has to find a new place to live. You're deprived of your familiar things and your familiar haunts. Then, of course, being the initiator of the separation, you bear the load of hostility from other people. All our friends clustered around my wife and suddenly I stopped being invited out. Then there's the financial hardship of it. I had nothing. The only thing I took with me was my stereo set, and I had to get furniture and dishes and all that sort of thing. From a very comfortable standard of living I was like a penniless student. I had one knife and one fork and one spoon. It was a damn miserable time, I must say."

Apart from the material discomforts and sometimes social pressure, an ex-husband carries with him all the leftovers of his marriage—the unresolved guilt feelings, doubt, resentment, and uncertainty, and these problems will be an added burden, another strain, on a relationship. In short, if a mistress is involved in a marriage breakdown, she will herself experience much of the agony and heartache of the breakdown, and her relationship with her lover will be inescapably affected. It is not uncommon for a mistress, having existed primarily to augment a marriage, or to act as a cushion when he takes his initial jump, to find herself cast out when the marriage is over, or at least to find the relationship deteriorating rapidly once her lover is "free."

Thus, while a number of women—one in particular coined herself the "interim woman"—had been involved with men who had left their wives during the course of the affair, only one relationship had survived the breakdown and evolved into a permanent relationship—and that still bore the scars of the anguished transition. The consummation of his "grand passion" in a second marriage had never taken place. He and his mistress had reverted to a situation where they lived separate lives, in separate apartments, seeing each other only as often as they had when they were lovers enjoying the intensity, fantasy and excitement of an illicit affair.

The Sexual Partner

Joanne Small is thirty-four and attractive in a modest, unassuming way. She commutes to work (for a magazine), is a mother of two, and lives a retiring suburban existence outside office hours.

"He'd been my husband's friend for as long as our marriage. I was used to seeing him around the house, used to him dropping in for meals. I was even used to the friendly hug, the kiss on the cheek that friendship brings. He was living in a relatively happy way with a woman, but it was a relationship I didn't appreciate then. It was a nonpossessive relationship. They both had freedom to do as they chose—and as she didn't particularly have much in common with us she very rarely visited.

"He and my husband were 'the boys' together—Peter Pans in pursuit of the hangover, the experience that would make them laugh, give them new jokes to add to their vast boring repertoire. I must admit that I didn't like either of them very much, especially after the birth of my third child. I had terrible baby blues and the physical effort of looking after three children under five years and a husband on shift-work depressed me physically as well as mentally.

"I used to drive him to work every day, but I got so behind in organizing myself that I'd just throw my coat over my nightie, comb my hair and we were ready to go. I can't remember ever wanting to get out of my nightie. I was so short of sleep all I wanted to do was to be ready to sleep when I could.

"My husband had not been the right lover for me for most of the years of our marriage. He usually had to have been drinking to get an erection. I got quite neurotic about the way he'd arrive home in the middle of the night all beery-breathed. First there'd be the hand that would slide across from the other side of the bed, then it would sort of run up and down my side. If I turned away he'd pull me toward him—never saying a word. Sometimes he'd kiss me, and often his breath was so awful I'd turn away. He was never really deterred. He'd just press on till he came. I can remember now how much it hurt. He never took time to arouse me, so there was no lubricating response from me. He never asked me what I felt.

"He started going away more and more often on jobs—or whatever. At least he wasn't coming home for days on end. I spent most of my time reading when I wasn't with the children, and in the library I found as many books on sex and sexual technique that I could. I read them continually, searching for a way to get pleasure. From the descriptions I realized I'd never had an orgasm. I had strange dreams at night about masturbation and on waking I remembered how as a child of fourteen I'd slept with a pillow between my legs and how I'd rubbed up and down against it. I started experimenting but I felt too embarrassed, too guilty to go on. I think in fact I was frightened by the way my body responded.

"One night my husband's friend came by to pick up some do-it-yourself equipment. He brought a bottle of wine with him, which we drank while waiting for my husband to arrive from work. When he got there it was after midnight and I offered to drive my husband's friend home. My husband staggered off to bed and we drove off.

"My husband's friend suddenly said, 'Why don't you wear make-up like you used to? You used to be very pretty. Now you don't seem to care.' I was very offended. It had nothing to do with him. When we stopped in front of his house, he leaned across to kiss me, and even though it sounds like fiction, I turned toward him and he kissed me on the nose. We both laughed and then he kissed me properly. I felt something like a chord inside me tighten, a pleasurable tightening that made me want more. He said, 'I'll come and see you next Tuesday,' and that's the way it began.

"All the words I'd read in books suddenly had meaning. Cunnilingus, fellatio, orgasm. He pulled the couch mattress on the living-room floor in front of the fire and he made love to me so beautifully—I'd never felt so free. I think for the first time I realized what sensuality meant and how much a woman can play a part in intercourse. I was so used to my husband's making me believe that it only had full pleasure for men that I was quite shaken by my experience.

"The whole of the next year was fraught with tension and unbelievable joy. My sex life with my husband satisfied him simply because when the shifting hand made its maneuver across the bed, I'd immediately think of his friend and feel wet. Nothing much else changed. Daily, in a domestic sense, I remained a slut. I did not want to look good. I made no attempt to do anything out of the ordinary. Nights were different. When my lover was visiting I made up, dressed up, cleaned the house, even cooked meals for us to have later. Quite often they were never eaten. He was as obsessed by me as I was by him and we preferred to play sex games for as long as we could.

"In company we were as cool as ever, though it took a great deal of control on my part. For the first time in my life I felt coquettish, and wanted to be noticed. I suddenly found other men aware of me, too, and they paid me compliments, believing that it was motherhood that made me flushed, more congenial.

"Some days I would arrange for a neighbor to have the children and spend the afternoon with him at his place, but most of the time he came to my house. Miraculously the children never woke—perhaps it has something to do with a mother's mind concentrating on something else. When we made love I wasn't a mother, or a wife; I was a mistress. I was quite abandoned, and continually surprised myself by my reactions to him.

"He was very good about letting me talk after we'd made love—something I'd never known before. And this was the time we became friends. We laughed together, enjoyed each other. We never talked about my husband, because we both had our own relationship with him to cope with. He still had his friendship and drinking bouts with him, and this could have gone on forever. For fourteen months it was magnificent; then the woman he lived with left him. He was quite shattered. Even though my marriage was rocky and unlikely to go on, he didn't see any reason to be the cause of the break-up.

"He decided to emigrate to Australia. We weren't in love—our feelings for each other were based on sex, and although we were very close there wasn't much else to keep a relationship going. He was as insecure as I was, and we would never have made partners except in bed. I was very sad to see him go, but the legacy he'd left me was an awareness of myself that could never be denied again.

"In those months I had with him, I felt I was a mistress. I sought and gave pleasure, which is what I imagine an old-fashioned mistress did. The gain was not in monetary terms, but in realization of self, and that's something money can't buy—unless of course you have intensive psychiatric treatment. And where's the pleasure in that?

"My marriage struggles on, but only because of the children. We both have our freedom now, and so really the marriage is unnecessary for any reason other than convenience. He still doesn't understand that sex can be enjoyed equally by a woman. He has what I call a Victorian outlook, which presumes that a woman is there only for a man's pleasure. I think I would welcome him meeting someone who could teach him differently. I can't—he just doesn't turn me on that way."

Sex is almost invariably the single most important ingredient in an affair. Most of the relationships of the mistresses and lovers we interviewed began with a sexual attraction, and for all but nine remained an extremely important aspect of an affair, getting better as long as the affair proceeded smoothly and without crisis (and sometimes even afterward).

All the men said sex with their mistresses was infinitely better than with their wives, while twenty of the mistresses explained they had experienced orgasm for the first time through their relationship with a married man. The six women who did not think their sex had got better as the affair developed put this deterioration down to the fact that through the years of their long relationships (one had lasted ten years, none less than three) sex had gradually become as "boring as any husband's and wife's."

"For a couple of years sex was passionate. Then a sort of married love developed between us, and sex

gradually became less pleasant and infrequent. Like most marriages, I suppose."

In addition, three masochists, who felt their "lousy sex" was a necessary part of their affairs, remained sexually dissatisfied.

Many who, at the beginning of the relationship, had seen their liaisons as only temporary were surprised that the sexual and other aspects developed as they did. The majority of men and women in our sample maintained that as the relationships developed, the sexual relationship became far and away the most important and pleasurable in their lives—if not the mainstay of the relationship itself. One married mistress explained:

"I have a lover for sexual reasons only. Sex in my marriage became like one of the chores, like doing the dishes. I was a very staid person, but I discovered how different I was when someone paid me special attention. My lover and I agreed that we wouldn't fall in love or try and run off with each other or anything like that. We both have too many responsibilities, so we agreed to make it just a sexual thing, and it's been a great success. I've blossomed so much my husband keeps asking me if I'm having an affair. I can even deny it without feeling guilty because I'm not a threat to anybody's marriage."

The mistress-lover relationship offers a well-nigh ideal environment for the development of mutually enjoyable sexuality. The feelings of intensity and infatuation are sustained at a high pitch for long periods of time—particularly when lovers meet exclusively to make love. Time is important, too, because they can never see enough of each other to make going to bed a boring ritual. Unlike the relationship of a single man and a woman, which normally encompasses all sorts of activities such as meeting friends, going to the movies, and so on, before eventually spending the night together, frequently the mistress and lover feel that time is so short they prefer to spend it exclusively in bed.

"We never wanted to go anywhere except to our apartment. There seemed to be such a short time, so much to say, and so little time to make love. A third party would have been intrusive."

The clandestine nature of such a relationship often enhances feelings of sexual excitement and anticipation. Secrecy encourages intimacy and an atmosphere where, it seems, fantasy and lack of inhibition can develop unchecked.

"It was all fun. We used to pretend we were different people from history. The apartment where we met became the Taj Mahal, the White House, the hot desert, the jungles of Brazil. We played a different game each time and it all revolved around the bed. There was no yesterday and no tomorrow. The world was only the apartment."

Another mistress described how endless sexual experimentation had become a cornerstone of their affair:

"He wants me to go through the book, and thats o.k. with me. He asks me to do things he'd never ask his wife to do—like troilism or group sex. He is really grateful that I agree to do these things. If he's a dirty old man then I'm a dirty old woman because I enjoy it too. He's proud of my

ability in bed and he wants to show me off by having others there. With me he can have fanatasies he can bring into the relationship. We use each other in a kind of partnership. He's terribly concerned about whether he satisfies me and takes a great deal of trouble to make sure he does."

Feelings of obligation being, initially at least, absent, and lovemaking totally voluntary, many will go to extraordinary lengths to be able to make love—dissembling, postponing dates, reorganizing arrangements—and making themselves up to increase their potential sexual appeal:

"I found myself making certain my toenails and fingernails were always clean. I bought all sorts of different-colored underwear—I couldn't go past a shop without going in to see if there was anything new and pretty on the market. I even bought a couple of sexy negligées and threw out my old robe. I wanted to feel glamorous."

Some mistresses mentioned how, before the arrival of their lovers, they would spend hours in the bathroom perfuming themselves to make their bodies enticing. The lovers in turn, they felt, became more considerate, devoting a great deal of time to foreplay and the general creation of an exciting atmosphere. The consequence for many was a greatly awakened sexual drive. Many women described themselves aroused to an extent never experienced before—emphasizing that this was made possible by the emotional as well as the sexual feelings involved.

"The whole relationship was rewarding for both of us because it was so beautiful. Every feeling is heightened, and one is extended as a person. That's the reward of an affair–though you're often not aware of it at the time.

"Everything in our sexual relationship was acceptable to me. I had never had an orgasm before I knew him–that was the thing that really came as a shock to me. I thought of us as a mystic union, and I used to get annoyed when after we'd made love he'd have a cigarette. It was almost like smoking in church."

Another mistress confessed:

"I had my first orgasm with him, and it came as a shock to me. I was physically incapable of moving during it, and as a woman proud of her independence I felt he'd found a way to dominate me. I was quite resentful of this power until I understood that I had as much power over him when he had an orgasm. After this discovery I was no longer overwhelmed."

The notion of a mistress existing solely to give her lover pleasure appears to be a thing of the past. It was important to the majority of mistresses we interviewed that they were as sexually fulfilled as were their lovers. Far from being a passive object, a man's plaything, the modern mistress, like the modern woman, is more and more an active, equally participating sexual partner:

"Our sexual interest in each other was so intense that there were times when we didn't know who was female and who was male. We both felt equal in the dominant role."

Even when a mistress feels she's being "used" in other

aspects of a relationship, often she will be sustained by a good sexual relationship:

"Even though I knew I ought to end the whole thing I became so obsessed with his body, I dreaded the thought that we would never again make love."

While for one man sexual relations with his wife had improved because of his greater arousal, five found the reverse to be true. Sex with their wives seemed by comparison an unpalatable duty they felt obliged to perform:

"I have an intense sex life with my mistresses, whereas I don't desire my wife sexually at all. I'll knock her off occasionally in the morning if I find I wake up with an erection, but I'm not sexually attracted to her anymore. She's always wanting more sex, but normally I get home so late I'm exhausted—and she does complain."

One man explained it was only through imagining his mistress that he could manage an erection with his wife:

"We only make love every few weeks now. I don't want her to think that I'm frustrated or looking elsewhere for sex, yet I don't enjoy making love to her anymore. In fact I have to pretend I'm with my mistress to make sex with my wife possible."

Sex then is vitally important to an affair. Yet even when it seems to be the fuel of a relationship, it is rarely enough to keep an affair going for a long period of time. Usually, unless a deep emotional relationship develops alongside the sexual relationship, the affair slowly diminishes. Similarly, where sexuality ceases, an affair is likely to end—or at least change into a different kind of "friendship":

"When his wife found out, we decided we had better be more discreet. We gave up sleeping together and instead met once a week in a bar. The whole character of the relationship changed when we stopped making love, and we became just like old friends."

Where sex gradually deteriorated, as was the case with a number of women whose mounting feelings of resentment, bitterness and anger prevented them from enjoying sex with their lovers any longer, the relationship rapidly went downhill.

The Mistress Behind the Man

Martha Wilson dresses in conservative flannel tweeds, looks and acts like an aging schoolmistress. She is always sweet, pleasant, and congenial. She works as a secretary.

"I can honestly say I have never regretted not being married. I think I have reaped far more rewards being a mistress than I would ever have had as a wife. In a material sense I am very well off, I can go where I want when I want, and there is no one preventing me being myself.

"When you've been involved in a relationship as long as I have, looking back to how it started is like asking an old married woman to remember her courting days. I know that I wasn't like the girls I went to school with. They wanted only to be married and to have children. I was never interested in either of these, but I think I assumed I would get married one day.

"I came from a very small Welsh village and I wanted more than anything to get away from it. I taught myself shorthand and typing and moved to Cardiff where I got a job in a factory. I was nineteen and I stayed there for two years. A big London firm took over the business and when one of the bosses asked if I'd like to join the staff there I jumped at the chance.

"I'd only been working there about six months when I was transferred to the director's suite—and that's where

I've been ever since. No, *I'm* not a director, but in decision-making terms I have the same power.

"The director I went to work for was ten years older than me, and I became used to being more than just a secretary. I used to arrange his cocktail parties, act as hostess when necessary, go with him to other cities on business trips. Right from the start I'd realized that I was attracted to his way of life, and I was attracted to him.

"We started going out to dinner when we'd worked late, and then when we went to Birmingham for a conference, we began sleeping together. His wife had been away for several weeks at their cottage in France, but I don't think that was the reason we slept together. We were a good working team and we both felt quite natural spending out-of-work hours together.

"Gradually I started making decisions for him when he was away from the office. I not only composed his letters, I started signing them as well—I knew instinctively he would agree with whatever decision I'd made. They weren't earth-shattering decisions but quite important for the firm.

"I'd been living in a small flat, and my boss insisted that I get a larger one and the firm would take care of the rent. This worked out well, for it was not only used for small business dinners but it also gave my lover and me a meeting place. I liked playing hostess at those dinners. It meant no work for me because a caterer did it all. As the dinners were usually for visiting businessmen, I was the only woman there and I enjoyed it.

"I was continually getting raises in pay so I could afford to buy really good clothes, and each year I started taking two weeks' holiday in first-class hotels. France was the place I liked best, because there were usually at least two unattached men who would be able to take me to dinner, sailing or sightseeing.

"The love affair with my boss continued to develop. He was very attached to me emotionally but he also needed me as part of his job. I met his wife quite frequently and we got on well. She only came up to London to shop or meet friends. She had her own life but she got what she wanted out of the marriage. Her sons were all at boarding school so she had a lot of freedom.

"At one time my lover became very guilty about the affair. He felt he wasn't doing right either by his wife or by me and he wanted to get a divorce and marry me. I felt that would be very silly because I was already seeing more of him than she was, and I certainly had all the influence over him I wanted. It took him a while to understand that as I considered myself his wife there was no need to have a legal tie. We both knew that if I became his wife I wouldn't be able to go on working for him and that I would be relegated to the house in the country. It certainly wouldn't suit me, and I convinced him that it wouldn't suit him either. He genuinely did do a lot of traveling around, and I just couldn't be a wife who sat and waited.

"We are always circumspect at the hotels wherever we go. We both have double rooms but usually adjoining or nearby. I like being with him, it makes me feel important. We never get bored in each other's company because we have so much in common. We share much more than we ever would in a marriage.

"On several occasions I've met other businessmen who travel with their personal assistants. They seem so much younger than I am, and I get the feeling that these women would all like to be the wife. I'd like to take them aside and tell them to hold on tight to what they have because being a wife will only mean loneliness. Perhaps I might have wished to marry if I'd wanted children. But I am too married to my job and my boss to want children. They would only have upset a perfect situation."

The mistress past and present has occasionally wielded an enormous power. Emma Hamilton, for example, came close to changing the course of history when she almost held Nelson back from Trafalgar. Mme. de Pompadour, mistress of Louis XV, exercised enormous power and influence in France for twenty years as "the uncrowned Queen of France." A brilliant, shrewd woman, at one time she was reputed to have run most of the internal business of France from her royal apartments.

From bourgeois French origins, Mme. de Pompadour was educated and groomed for her role by a determined mother who saw marriage as a deadly serious maneuver for upward mobility. Possessing all the ingredients for social success, attractive, elegant, and sociable, she was installed, after a fortunate "social" marriage and a great deal of conniving, as Louis's royal mistress in 1745, and remained in the king's favor until she died.

Martha Wilson, who, like Mme. de Pompadour, had turned the situation to her own advantage, enjoyed the role she found for herself and worked only toward making herself indispensable and irreplaceable as far as her lover was concerned. Having come to rely on his mistress without being put in a position where he would feel guilty, a man would undoubtedly be reluctant to alter the status quo.

One can only speculate about the influence Marguerite (Missy) LeHand had where Franklin D. Roosevelt was concerned. She was his mistress, according to his son, both when he was governor of New York and when he was President of the United States—a period of about twenty years.

It is ironic how many leading political figures—the so-called guardians of public morality—have had long-term, illicit relationships which would have scandalized the public—divorce being, in these instances, out of the question. In Britain the longstanding relationship that Prime Minister Lloyd George maintained with Frances Stevenson was, apparently, respected even by his bitterest opponents. In 1912 Lloyd George invited her to become a secretary to the Treasury "on his own terms which were in direct conflict with my essentially Victorian upbringing," she wrote in *The Years That Are Past*. She accepted these terms, and so began a relationship that ended only with Lloyd George's death in 1945.

Frances Stevenson not only loved Lloyd George, according to A. J. P. Taylor, but she also shared his political interests and was at home in the political world. She helped him compose his speeches and acted as a political sounding board. She went with him on important foreign missions and met the leading statesmen of the day. On Lloyd George's behalf she negotiated with the press lords, Northcliffe and Beaverbrook, writing down everything that was said. She was always on hand to listen, praise, even to give advice when asked. Lloyd George and Frances Stevenson eventually married—in 1943—two years before he was created earl. He died two months later. For all the important years of his political life Frances Stevenson had played a powerful role, a role that a wife in those days could not play.

Lady Jennie Churchill became notorious with her

pursuit of power—for her husband and son—through her lovers. As the beautiful American wife of Lord Randolph Churchill, she took advantage of the social position offered her wherever and whenever she could, becoming socially and politically influential through her knowledge of the right people. Given Lord Randolph's syphilitic condition, her marriage became one of social convenience, based on an unspoken arrangement: Jennie could have her suitors, Randolph his friends.

She played a valuable role in her husband's political life, helping to write his speeches, campaigning around the country for him. She was the unrecognized fifth member of the political group called the Fourth Party, which consisted of Lord Randolph, Arthur Balfour, Sir Henry Wolff and John Gorst. Not only was she favored by a future prime minister, she was also entertained by a future king. Prince Edward gave her expensive jewelry and invited her to be a frequent guest at Sandringham—and Randolph did not always accompany her.

When Lord Randolph finally succumbed to the debilitating disease, Lady Jennie concentrated on helping her son Winston. As Ralph G. Martin, Jennie's biographer, wrote, she would "tap the men and open the doors to prepare the complicated pattern of stepping stones to his future."

From our interviews it would seem that some modern mistresses also wish to get involved with whatever business their lovers are in. Three of the mistresses interviewed experienced power in this behind-the-scenes way—and learned a great deal from it.

"I came to know everything there is to know about publishing. For ten years he used to discuss his problems with me and I often helped him make up his mind about a

The Mistress Behind the Man

book he wasn't sure about. *He was very successful as a publisher, and I know that he never discussed his work with his wife. Just with me."*

Only when this relationship ended did this mistress turn the knowledge she gained to her own advantage. With his help she established a publicity firm which has since prospered.

Another mistress, who had lived with a writer for several years, started helping him with his work because she was interested in it. His was a specialist field and she discovered she was better than he at expressing his thoughts.

"We established a routine: I wrote two books for him, did all his typing, wrote his lectures. In fact I earned quite a lot of our money. I even helped to support his wife. I don't think at the beginning he meant to use me, but we became such a good partnership that he wanted it to go on."

When her lover's infidelity brought the liaison to an end, the mistress kept up her professional attachment to her former lover; they have now established a business and, although as a ghost writer she doesn't receive any more recognition than in the past, she now benefits financially.

Airlines was the meeting ground for a twenty-six-year-old public relations worker and her lover. This mutual interest gave them a base for the advancement of their affair, which had started out as "a little fling." They found themselves at the same international centers and gradually they became more involved with each other.

"He's very wealthy, very powerful and highly respected. I was extremely flattered by his attention. He

told me he could offer me job security, love, money—everything except marriage. And this would continue whether or not I got married."

For this mistress the future holds a lucrative business partnership with her lover, so she accepts the limits of the relationship. And there are compensations. Because they have the same work interest they can spend working hours together. And her position is recognized.

"*We go out openly with his friends and business associates because it's accepted in these circles. When we go out with clients they're mostly with their own mistresses anyway. I'm more surprised in this business to find someone who's not involved than to meet someone with another woman.*"

She has been quick to realize that a liaison with such a powerful man can be only for her good. Knowing him has increased not only her self-esteem but also her esteem in the eyes of her employers.

"*They all know about me, and I see them looking at me and thinking: if she can get this man she must have something.*"

For a woman to reap such rewards from the "power game" she needs to be temperamentally complementary to her lover—that is, she must understand his business or political world, recognize and respect his role, and devote herself to *his* progress. Should she, at any moment, step out from his shadow and attempt to play an equal or dominant role, she will have violated the unspoken rules of the game, probably jeopardizing the relationship.

Thus, while there will always be some women content to stay behind the scenes, like Martha Wilson, perceiving all her needs to be met by her employer-lover, this type of mistress will probably rapidly become obsolete as women seek to become powerful in their own right. While many women will undoubtedly continue to involve themselves in liaisons with powerful men, some for emotional reasons, others for material benefit, all indications suggest that the altruistic mistress who devotes herself to a man without even being rewarded the status of wife is on the way out.

The Predator

Elizabeth Farmer is thirty-eight, petite, dynamic (some would say aggressive). She works as a journalist, dresses with flair, talks non-stop and seduces men relentlessly and with ease.

"I have a basic attitude—I've been used so often by men that it's my turn to use them. I will only go out with a man who can be of use to me, who can assist me with my career. I'm a late-starting journalist, so I only go for men who are right at the top. At my age starting on a lower rung would be a waste of time. As every editor I've ever met is married, I have to become a mistress to them. The one-night stand has no value, as I'm not doing this for sex.

"My strategy at the beginning was quite simple. When I moved from California to New York I had press accreditation from quite an influential paper for whom I had been doing freelance work. In New York I went through the telephone book and phoned the editors of a number of the newspapers listed. I told them I wanted to interview them. I've found that everyone—successful men especially—likes to be interviewed. They feel flattered. If they sounded at all hesitant I would say, "I think you should meet me. I'm quite attractive." It never failed. They expected a femme fatale and they got one. I swept into the interviews and set about impressing them. In the course of the interview I would mention that I was looking for a job, and they almost always responded. I was given special treatment.

"I decided I would try to seduce the most handsome and influential of the men I interviewed—and the most responsive one, of course. I singled out just one. We had only two meals together before I became his mistress.

"I'd worked out how to play the game. I knew how to imply subtly there were other lovers (and there were) to make him jealous and competitive—I have a sneaking suspicion that this is the only hunting spirit left in men like this. I knew how to imply I was more successful than I was. I name-dropped furiously and in the beginning manipulated every situation. It worked. Within five months of arriving in New York I was living in a magnificent apartment and I had two men helping me. The apartment is paid for by my married lover of four years' standing from California, but I'm being kept by my other lover. He knows that someone else exists in my life but not that he's paying for my apartment. My apartment is really luxurious and it gives me importance and adds mystery as far as my new lover is concerned.

"I intend keeping the relationship going until I am well established. At the moment my lover makes sure I get all my articles published. I'll gradually meet other men, find other outlets, but in the meantime I'm sitting pretty.

"I'm carefully collecting contacts. I'm not promiscuous—that way, men use you. No, my style is to flirt madly with influential men and tantalize them as much as I can. Only long-standing relationships will help me benefit careerwise.

"Why did I start out doing this? Because I've been married twice and both times I have been badly hurt. One of them left me for another woman, and both left me without any money. The second marriage was a pure mistake—he gave me nothing, physically, emotionally or financially. I was pretty miserable for a while, and then I got mad. I took a long, hard look at myself.

"The only asset I had, I realized, was myself. I had intelligence and good looks on my side. I certainly didn't look thirty-eight. I completely discounted any idea of taking a minor secretarial job or even trying to join a local paper. I was determined that I was going to get the best job and, like an ad-man, I set out to sell myself. I guess I really regarded myself as a product, and I was a first-class saleswoman because I had everything to gain.

"I know that if I hadn't gone about it the way I did, I wouldn't be where I am now. I don't feel at all guilty about it, because long ago I realized that it was only because I was a woman that I had to go about establishing a career this way. I have nothing of my own, so I must get what I want from men.

"If I had been a man I would have had a good education and I wouldn't have spent eleven years as a housewife, wasting all my talents. I consider I'm getting my just deserts. I'm a women's liberation supporter, though I don't actively participate in the movement. I think we women have got to use every available weapon if we're going to get out of our subordinated condition. I've done it all on my own—by using the only resource I have—and presumably I've given my lovers something as well, or they wouldn't have hung around for so long and wouldn't have given me so much in return. I enjoy this new attitude. It means I'm always winning, instead of losing as I did for all the years I was married."

The cold, calculating mistress-on-the-make does exist: if anything she appears to be on the increase, as women abandon the traditional pose of altruism and seek to hustle their way into the professional rat race. The numbers of women we spoke to who had used an affair for purposes of "upward mobility" were quite startling—as was the number of women who, like Elizabeth Farmer, were prepared to explain quite honestly what they were about.

One of the mistresses, who had risen from the position of secretary to that of managing director of a small office, said that her transformation from a woman who was used by men to one who used them resulted from her increasing honesty:

"It's only that I admit what I'm doing now, and no longer try to rationalize my behavior with altruistic deception. I realize that altruism is inherently selfish anyhow—I was using my studied selflessness as a way of getting and keeping a man. Nowadays I just make quite sure that nobody is taking me for granted. I sit down and say, What's in it for me? What's in it for him? And make sure that neither party is ripping the other off."

A "femme fatale" of twenty-five had undergone a similar "awakening."

"I realized that every boss I had I was going to sleep with, so I thought I might as well get some boss who was really wealthy and prepared to pay for his pleasure."

Another's "enlightenment" had come through bitter experience:

"I was very naïve at eighteen. I was working in my first job, as a secretary in a publishing house, when my

boss told me that if I slept with him I could get a promotion. He said if I didn't he would tell the agency I had stolen money. I was so scared of him that I agreed. He was just using me. Eventually I wrote a letter to the managing editor and the bastard got sacked. He was always threatening me, and I turned the tables on him. He taught me one thing—no man will ever use me again."

An increasing number of women, particularly American women, seem to resist the idea of sleeping with a married man without material reward—though the reward itself varies a great deal. Only two women we interviewed had, like Elizabeth Farmer, consciously sought out men for their professional usefulness. More common were women who saw manifest material advantages in entering into a relationship with some man who appealed to them, the advantages being just one of a number of attractions. Thus, one woman had put herself through college with the help of her lover. Another had made her debut into the New York jetset. Several had risen with alacrity in their professions, and a number had sumptuous apartments paid for by their lovers. Another had embarked upon a successful political career in Washington through her long-standing relationship with a leading American senator. (She said she had many friends who had used similar launching pads into Washington politics.)

"I wanted to use him because he knew everybody in New York, and, it often seemed, everybody who was anybody in the entire United States. I wanted to move into the big, jetsetting society, and he was my vehicle. We'd go away to people's estates, trot off on glamorous weekends to the Bahamas, go out practically every night when he was in New York to glamorous parties where

Tennessee Williams and Danny Kaye would be. His marriage was really packing up, so he made no excuses about me—in fact he rather showed me off. I was quite a hit in that milieu, being younger, and very different. They thought I was quite glamorous. The whole time I was going out with him I was looking for a rich, handsome boyfriend. I liked him—I felt comfortable with him—but certainly I was in no sense in love with him. Apart from searching in those circles for the right single man, I was getting a massive ego-boost. If I was with somebody important, I felt important myself. Everybody loved him and wanted him, which made me feel fantastic. Ironically, the connections I made through him don't remember me now—or if they do, only as the girlfriend of so-and-so, nothing more."

Another woman enjoyed the expensive gifts her lover continually showered her with:

"Every week two enormous bunches of flowers would arrive at my apartment—he had a standing order with the florist for two dozen red roses every week—and every other week I would get solid gold trinkets from Cartier's, Steuben Glass ornaments—and the like. It was like having an all-year Santa Claus—irresistible. We would lunch at Lutèce and "21," go to the opera and do all those things I could never afford to do myself. In addition, I grew to be quite fond of him, so it was almost a perfect set-up."

Said another:

"I knew through him I could find a whole new way of life that otherwise I would have had difficulty getting involved in. He introduced me to an enormous number of *interesting, useful people who helped me when I left college. I had no desire to break up his marriage, just to get launched in my new career."*

There is, then, considerable variety in the practical benefits certain women look for in an affair. The greatest extreme is the mistress who eschews emotional involvement altogether and plays the market for the highest stakes. Her emotions are involved only to the extent that she knows how best to use them for effect. She plans her affairs as a guerrilla would plan an assault on an enemy. With her eye fixed on material reward, she taps her conquests for gifts that will appreciate in value: jewelry, houses, real estate and furs. Subtly she plays upon her lovers' feelings of guilt, inducing them to compensate her handsomely for the "privilege" of having an affair.

In this respect she resembles the Victorian kept woman, who believed in being a financial parasite—with just one difference. The Victorian kept woman usually had no other means of support. This sort of mistress simply does not choose to try.

It would appear that such women are invariably those with little self-respect or belief in their capacity to love and be loved. Not believing that mutuality or emotional reciprocity is possible in a relationship, they seek a transaction. Since they do not believe themselves capable of being rewarded with love or deep affection, they fall back on the more shallow and ultimately transient rewards of material abundance.

More common, though, were other mistresses who, in varying degrees, resembled a particular type of woman described by Toni Woolf: someone who "is independent, self-contained, primarily concerned with her own achievements; who lives life like a man and who is in danger of misusing human relationships as a means of business or for the sake of a career."

There is no doubt that as women become more career conscious and independent, they will increasingly come to assess their relationships in terms of how they will benefit from them. It would be misleading, however, to categorize all women who put their self-interest first as "predators." For, after all, they are only doing what men have always been expected to do.

Only the cynical woman who represses all emotion in the name of self-advancement, or who chooses a man simply for his material potential, can properly be called a predator. Such a woman who, whether out of unconscious revenge, inability to love, or sheer ambition, uses her position simply to use men, represents an ironic inversion of the classic mistress role. The mistress was assumed to live for men, to satisfy *their* needs, but the predator, by deftly swapping roles, has learned how to exploit her subordinate position in order to dominate or control men, and to get her own (material at least) needs continuously satisfied.

The Free Agent

Susan Redding is blonde, statuesque and striking. At twenty-six having "frittered away" (she now says) six years of her working life as a secretary, she is now training to be a social worker. A recent convert to feminism, she is active in the movement, speaking and organizing, and attending "consciousness-raising" groups.

"Until I became involved with my present lover, I had always revolved my life around men. But this relationship began at the same time as I started to get interested in the Women's Liberation Movement. I was able to use my lover as a guinea pig in a sense.

"I took things to extremes. I wouldn't go near the kitchen when he was around, or wait for him if he turned up late. Initially this caused quite a bit of conflict, because his previous women had been sort of substitute wives who fluttered around him, cooked for him any hour of the day of night, and generally waited on him hand and foot. They were sexy lap dogs and they had no lives of their own except what he offered them.

"Naturally he had grown to expect this treatment as a lover's prerogative. He would turn up at two in the morning and ask for mushrooms on toast. When he'd eaten he'd just sit there waiting for me to jump up and wash the dishes.

"When I explained that I just wasn't going to put up with it, he was shocked at first, but after that I think it was the thing that fascinated him more than anything else. He became intrigued by the life I led. The more independent I became the more clinging he became.

"He told me the second time we met that he was married. I didn't mind at all. I didn't want to marry him so it didn't matter. If I had wanted to marry him I suppose I would have cared, but this way there was no struggling with guilt or wrestling with a conscience. I knew that if it wasn't me it would be someone else.

"I've never believed a mistress can break up a happy marriage. His wasn't good then but I think it's a little better now just because he's having a good time sexually and intellectually. He always felt deprived in these areas in his marriage but now he goes home a happier person and therefore a better husband.

"In some ways it has been a godsend that he is married. In fact I think it was the saving grace of our relationship, because he hasn't been able to put many of the pressures on me that otherwise he might have. He would have wanted to move in with me. I would have refused and he would have seen this refusal as a sign of rejection. Because he has accepted the fact that I don't want to marry him or live with him, our relationship has survived.

"I see as much of him as I want, and there are times when I am pleased to tell him to go back to his wife and family. At one stage, when he was talking about how neurotic his daughter was becoming, I insisted he spend more time at home.

"But I don't want to know about his wife and kids. They don't figure in my life or get in the way of our relationship. I never hear him say, 'I've got to get home to the wife.' Perhaps if I did I might resent her, but in fact she never impinges on us at all. I'm only interested in her as an objective study of what happens to women housebound in a marriage, and to that extent I feel sorry for her.

"My lover has told me that she is the product of a strict Catholic upbringing. She wouldn't use contraceptives and so she got kids she didn't want and became permanently tied to the house. She's lost all confidence in herself. Before her marriage she showed promise as an actress, and she could obviously try and start again, but she can't leave the security of the home even to audition.

"I don't think she knows about me because her husband often has to work through the night in his job. She is used to the routine of his being out five nights a week. In some ways I suspect she is relieved he is away so much. He says she never makes any fuss about it.

"I know I am a symptom of failure in his marriage, every sort of failure. For both of them it seems a disastrous marriage. He didn't want children in the first place, so now he doesn't like them. He longs to have a child he has planned. The sex between him and his wife is nonexistent because she is afraid of becoming pregnant again. They have no mental communication at all. He's had hundreds of girlfriends through the years. He wants to leave her and I am sure he will when he can afford it financially.

"I've had two experiences with married men before this. The first was my first sexual experience and it was quite important to me. Both affairs lasted about six months and I learned a lot about sex. They were older than I was, were very good teachers and not fumbling amateurs—which is what a young woman needs when she wants to find out what it's all about.

"The relationship with my present lover has been going for nearly eighteen months and it has been really important to me. I have learned a lot through it. I have learned that relationships with men are much better if a woman retains her own life, her own interests and individuality. I'd never done that before.

"I can't see the relationship going on much longer, however. We're both ready for a change, and when the time comes there won't be any recriminations, soul-searching and guilt. It will end cleanly, because we've been honest with each other all the way through and neither has been possessive or demanding of the other.

"At the moment I'm too much in the process of growth to even consider getting married. I imagine I will want to some day when I'm more ready for it. I have definite career plans and I would never consider giving them up to take up a career as housewife.

"I am going to be financially independent whether I marry or not. I certainly would not live off a husband. My idea of marriage isn't the conventional orange-blossom idea—to me it just means living with somebody more or less permanently and sharing something with him. Not now though. I'm not prepared to take the risk until I'm a fully developed person."

In our interviews we came across a number of women who, under the influence of feminism, had begun to abandon the classically dependent posture of the mistress and to adopt, instead, an attitude toward the affair similar to that traditionally held by the male.

Like their lovers, these women had worlds of their own which existed independently of the affair. Many considered themselves liberated women and were no longer prepared to accept that their lovers' interests should have precedence over their own. Having their own friends, interests, goals and achievements, they could not subordinate themselves or sacrifice their interests for their lovers—or indeed, for any man. They did not try to prove their indispensability to their man by encouraging his dependence on them, and they eschewed the dangers of becoming a "second wife." They regarded their lovers as being as independent and self-sufficient as they themselves were. Conceiving their affairs as relationships between equals, they viewed the independence, lack of deep commitment and partial attachment inherent in an affair as potential assets rather than as built-in disadvantages.

Feminism, obviously, has begun to penetrate and revolutionize the unrecognized, clandestine relationships of our society. In thus transforming the role of the mistress, the "free agent" has become something of a throwback to the hetaera or courtesan of ancient Greece. The hetaera, unlike the captive Grecian wife, was in an envied position; she was free to be educated, to grow and develop as an individual, even to select her own lovers, and act as an intellectual companion to them.

Having acknowledged that, it remained unclear to us—and, it seemed, to most of these women—why it was necessary to have an uninvolved, undemanding relationship with a *married* man, given that the world, we are often led to believe, is bursting with single men equally eager to enjoy casual relationships free of the commitments and responsibilities.

In general, it seemed that unconscious, irrational or purely personal factors—such as an attraction to older men—accounted for the initial involvement, which the women had then tried retrospectively and consciously to rationalize. On the other hand, some women simply had not managed to find single men with whom they felt they could pursue a casual and undemanding relationship. As one free agent explained:

"I find in the relationships I've had with married men that it is possible to have an emotional relationship without being saddled with the typical demands and obligations of an emotional involvement with a single man. All the single men I meet seem frantically looking for the ideal wife."

Another said:

"In most relationships with single men there comes a time when you either go and live together or you stop seeing each other. These sorts of pressures are absent when you're going out with a married man—you can just go out and enjoy it—you don't have to think of the future all the time."

Some even claimed it was sheer necessity:

"The single men I meet in the normal course of a day are either homosexuals, mother's boys or insecure men who are quite unable to cope with me. Being a mistress to a married man is the only alternative to being a hermit."

Most of the free agents we interviewed saw their involvements with married men as only temporary, occupying them in an arid period, rehabilitating them after a damaging, painful relationship, or simply as a convenient interlude which fitted in with a busy phase in a woman's life. None of them saw it as a desirable, permanent condition.

One free agent said:

"I am so busy at work and in developing myself at this stage of my life, I simply don't have the time and energy left for an intense relationship. Three nights a week are taken up with courses, psychoanalysis, group therapy, so it is ideal for me at this stage to have a lover who lives abroad and whom I see about once a month. I'm extremely fond of him. He is gentle, considerate and loving. He provides me with a sort of emotional base at this juncture of my life. I make absolutely no demands on him, nor he on me. We are 'free to be,' which is exactly what I need at the moment."

Another said:

"I had affairs with married men because it was so easy. There was no possibility of involvement. You can enjoy a relationship for the sake of it with no strings attached. Also it fitted into my lifestyle during that period. I was trying to reconstruct my life after a horrendously painful relationship. I needed a period of freedom from the hassles of an emotional attachment. The feeling that I was in control and independent was heady for a while, and very cathartic. Ultimately, however, I began to find relationships without commitment unfulfilling."

A woman whose affairs had always taken place in between deeper relationships described how she would always conclude an affair if something more permanent loomed on the horizon.

"I think the advantages of an affair depend on a woman's attitude toward it. If she can enjoy it in a

healthy way and not have expectations about marriage evolving from it, it can be great. The liaisons I've had with married men have all been in between relationships with single men which have been much more serious. During these arid periods it's great to have an affair, but I've ended them when single men came along."

Of all the women we interviewed, these free-agent mistresses were the only ones who were thoroughly reconciled to their mistress roles and who continually derived pleasure from their relationships. They remain, as yet, exceptions to the general rule.

Nevertheless, the balance even the most successful free agents had achieved always remained as precarious as a tightrope walker's. The affair was always in danger, despite all efforts to the contrary, of turning into a deeper emotional relationship than was initially intended. Several mistresses who had embarked on their affairs with what they imagined were independent, rational, "liberated" attitudes had gradually found themselves succumbing to irrational behavior and expectations as their emotional involvement intensified. Despite their continuing intellectual commitment to independence and personal responsibility, they still found themselves wanting to be dependent and possessed.

On the other hand, as one woman found to her dismay, a married man can become dependent, misjudge a mistress's feelings, or imagine that beneath the controlled façade are much deeper feelings than there actually are.

"Unfortunately he thinks he's in love with me, which makes it rather awkward. He moved into my apartment when I was overseas. He left his wife and just moved in, hoping to surprise me when I got back. This was something I had never bargained for, and far from feeling delighted I feel quite resentful at having my independence abruptly terminated like this. I'm not ready for a permanent or exclusive relationship yet."

Even where an apparently enduring balance is achieved, it is possible, as one free agent observed, that its achievement is predicated upon the exercise of a considerable degree of emotional control—a switching on and off of powerful emotions that can ultimately be very destructive.

"I see my lover about once a week. We have an ecstatic weekend, full of love and tenderness and feeling—then, on Sunday night when he leaves, I simply for my own sanity have to switch off all that tenderness and emotion, and plunge myself into the working world again. I have survived doing this for eighteen months now, but recently I've begun to wonder just what this turn-on, turn-off pattern is doing to my emotional well-being."

Thus even the successful free agent is always in a position that requires vigilance, self-control, and compromise, and that is always susceptible to the dangers inherent in every mistress-lover relationship. And the limitations she places on the affair normally preclude the development of a really satisfying relationship.

"Ultimately," one free agent ruefully concluded, "it's a non-relationship. A married man's first commitment to his wife and family make it impossible for him to give you what is needed to develop a full and loving relationship."

The Failure of Monogamy

The long extra-marital affair which runs parallel to a marriage can be seen as the Western equivalent of polygamy or concubinage. Seventy percent of the men in our sample required sexual fidelity of their wives and mistresses, proving themselves in this context little different than the polygamous Muslim husband.

Here the comparison ends, however, for the Western mistress is, in some respects, at a disadvantage compared to the second, third and fourth wives of a Muslim marriage who are granted the same (if restricted) rights as the first wife. The Western mistress operates entirely without social sanction. She remains in the shadows while society kneels before the altar of marriage. The monogamous lifetime relationship "till death do us part" is still the ideal, maintained by romantic propaganda and social conditioning. The divorce statistics and the widespread incidence of extra-marital affairs reveal the chasm between the romantic myth and everyday reality, and it is the mistress who often finds herself paying the price society extracts for papering over the cracks between romantic fiction and real life.

The mistress's relationship with her married lover takes place in a twilight world. The constant strain and duplicity the arrangement demands is the main reason it will probably endure only a year or two, even under comparatively favorable conditions. For society maintains the pretense of a successfully monogamous culture only by ensuring that the mistress remains "persona non grata."

Ironically, by keeping her a social outcast, we ensure that, like the prostitute, she is not only the victim of monogamy but its perpetrator as well. By ignoring her existence we ensure that while a mistress may threaten an individual marriage, she does not challenge the institution of marriage per se. Above all, we avoid confronting the implications of her role today. For, in fact, by her very existence she holds up a mirror to monogamy and exposes many of the hypocrisies, deceits and fallacies that marriage in Western culture depends upon for its survival. Indeed, her very existence begs the questions—Are men and women by nature monogamous? Can monogamous marriage endure much longer in its present form, based as it is on the assumption that love, for the majority of the population, occurs only once in every life and lasts a lifetime? This in spite of the fact that love continues to be presented by Madison Avenue as a spontaneous, irrational emotion that will overtake one constantly, as long as one uses the right toothpaste, hairspray, et cetera. From advertisements and popular literature, we are conditioned to expect that falling in love is a frequent occurrence, accompanied by blindness to reality.

Although, as Erich Fromm observes in *The Art of Loving*, the character of this sort of popularized love is more properly called infatuation, it is nevertheless the love we are conditioned to yearn for and expect as a prerequisite to supposedly lifetime monogamous marriage.

Until Victorian times the distinction between the legal character of marriage and the irrational condition of love was recognized and accepted. Marriage more often took place for reasons of convenience—property, dowry, inheritance—than for love. Today in the Western world we have tried to erase and ignore the contradiction between the legal character of marriage and the supposedly irrational nature of love. The mistress is a living example of how we have failed. Yet, ironically, her attainment of the Madison Avenue ideal of romantic love shows to what extent the contradiction continues.

What of the future of the extra-marital affair?

Like the institution of marriage, it is inevitably undergoing change. Inescapably subject to the social pressures of the times, it is not, and will not be, unaffected by the upheaval in values sweeping the Western world. It is noteworthy, for example, that the American mistresses interviewed for this book had a markedly clearer understanding of their predicament, and a stronger sense of identity, than did their British or "Commonwealth" peers. Much of the difference could be ascribed to the greater impact of feminism in the United States.

Undoubtedly, the effect of feminism will be felt both in the marriage of the man and in the life of the mistress, and will, therefore, ultimately transform the relationship of the mistress and her lover. A more relaxed attitude, both social and legal, toward divorce will tend to reduce the number of marriages that survive despite their obvious failure. The realization that children may well suffer more from a bad marriage than from an honest divorce will contribute as well. Above all, the growing desire of women to assert greater independence and to pursue personal growth—in short, to see themselves as individuals rather than as adjuncts of a man—will continue to alter many of the ground rules of modern mistresshood.

When men and women were prepared to sacrifice everything to preserve the form of marriage in the interests of social respectability, the mistress was the loser. In the future, it may be that men and women will be able to have relationships that are not crippled by the hypocrisies of society, as extra-marital affairs have almost inescapably been in the past. But it would be going too far to predict that the mistress will, imminently, come out as the winner. The imbalances inherent in an extra-marital affair may diminish with feminism, but they will not disappear. Even the free agent has to deal with this inescapable reality, and her "victory" (in an affair) is often as pyrrhic as that of the predator or the masochist.

Feminist theory, in short, does not detract from the practical reality of competition for men, a woman's unconscious search for a father figure, her preference for older (married) men, and all the other motives driving women into extra-marital affairs. It will, however, undoubtedly help the mistress develop a sense of independence and self-respect, which so many of the mistresses we interviewed so manifestly lacked.

WITHDRAWN
From Bertrand Library

HQ806 .K43   ABZ 8291

a 7535200010854 c